Meeting SEN
in the Curriculum:
MODERN FOREIGN LANGUAGES

Other titles in the Meeting Special Needs in the Curriculum series:

Meeting Special Needs in English
Tim Hurst
1 84312 157 3

Meeting Special Needs in Maths
Brian Sharp
1 84312 158 1

Meeting Special Needs in Citizenship
Alan Combes
1 84312 169 7

Meeting Special Needs in Religious Education
Dilwyn Hunt
1 84312 167 0

Meeting Special Needs in History
Richard Harris and Ian Luff
1 84312 163 8

Meeting Special Needs in Design and Technology
Louise Davies
1 84312 166 2

Meeting Special Needs in Art
Kim Earle and Gill Curry
1 84312 161 1

Meeting Special Needs in Music
Victoria Jacquiss and Diane Paterson
1 84312 168 9

Meeting Special Needs in ICT
Sally McKeown
1 84312 160 3

Meeting Special Needs in Science
Carol Holden
1 84312 159 X

Meeting Special Needs in Geography
Diane Swift
1 84312 162 X

Meeting Special Needs in PE and Sport
Crispin Andrews
1 84312 164 6

Meeting SEN
in the Curriculum:

MODERN FOREIGN LANGUAGES

Sally McKeown

David Fulton Publishers

For Maurice Court

David Fulton Publishers Ltd
The Chiswick Centre, 414 Chiswick High Road, London W4 5TF

www.fultonpublishers.co.uk

First published in Great Britain in 2004 by David Fulton Publishers

10 9 8 7 6 5 4 3 2 1

Note: the right of Sally McKeown to be identified as the author of this work has been
asserted by her in accordance with the Copyright, Designs and Patents Act 1988.

British Library Cataloguing in Publication Data
A catalogue record for this book is available from the British Library.

David Fulton Publishers is a division of Granada Learning, part of ITV plc.

ISBN 1 84312 165 4

Typeset by Servis Filmsetting Ltd, Manchester
Printed and bound in Great Britain

Contents

Acknowledgements

The author would like to thank:

Clare Martin, George Hastwell School, Cumbria
Elaine Hampson, West Oaks School, Boston Spa
Angela Fryer, Advisory Teacher ICT/SEN, Coventry
Jen Taylor, freelance consultant
David Stewart and pupils at Shepherd School, Nottingham
John Wheway and Learning Support Assistants at Mosley Park School, Bilston
Barry Kruger, Becta
Abby Rhodes, Becta
Mandy McCartney, Becta
Gail Haythorne, Head of MFL, Woldingham School, Surrey

Contributors to the Series

The author

Sally McKeown is responsible for language work in the Inclusion and SEN team at Becta. She has a particular interest in learning difficulties and dyslexia. She wrote the MFL Special Needs materials for the New Opportunities Fund (NOF) training for the Centre for Information on Language Teaching (CILT), and is author of *Unlocking Potential* and co-author of *Supporting Children with Dyslexia* (Questions Publishing). She writes regularly for the *TES*, *Guardian* and *Special Children* magazines.

A dedicated team of SEN specialists and subject specialists have contributed to the *Meeting Special Needs in the Curriculum* series.

Series editor

Alan Combes started teaching in South Yorkshire in 1967 and was Head of English at several secondary schools before taking on the role of Head of PSHE as part of being senior teacher at Pindar School, Scarborough. He took early retirement to focus on his writing career and has authored two citizenship text-books as well as writing several features for the TES. He has been used as an adviser on citizenship by the DfES and has emphasised citizenship's importance for special needs pupils as a speaker for NASEN.

SEN specialists

Sue Briggs is a freelance education consultant based in Hereford. She writes and speaks on inclusion, special educational needs and disability, and Autistic Spectrum Disorders and is a lay member of the SEN and Disability Tribunal. Until recently, she was SEN Inclusion Co-ordinator for Herefordshire Education Directorate. Originally trained as a secondary music teacher, Sue has extensive experience in mainstream and special schools. For six years she was teacher in charge of a language disorder unit.

Sue Cunningham is a Learning Support Co-ordinator at a large mainstream secondary school in the West Midlands where she manages a large team of Learning Support teachers and assistants. She has experience of working in both mainstream and special schools and has set up and managed a resource base for pupils with moderate learning difficulties in the mainstream as part of an initiative to promote a more inclusive education for pupils with SEN.

Sally McKeown is an Education Officer with Becta, the government funded agency responsible for managing the National Grid for Learning. She is responsible for the use of IT for learners with disabilities, learning difficulties or additional needs. She is a freelance journalist for the *Times Educational Supplement* and a regular contributor to disability magazines and to *Special Children* magazine. In 2001 her book *Unlocking Potential* was shortlisted for the NASEN Special Needs Book Award.

Subject specialists

English

Tim Hurst has been a special educational needs co-ordinator in five schools and is particularly interested in the role and use of language in teaching.

Science

Carol Holden works as a science teacher and assistant SENCO in a mainstream secondary school. She has developed courses for pupils with SEN within science and has gained a graduate diploma and MA in Educational Studies, focusing on SEN.

History

Richard Harris has been teaching since 1989. He has taught in three comprehensive schools, as history teacher, Head of Department and Head of Faculty. He has also worked as teacher consultant for secondary history in West Berkshire.

Ian Luff is Assistant Headteacher of Kesgrave High School, Suffolk and has been Head of History in three comprehensive schools.

Maths

Brian Sharp is a Key Stage 3 Mathematics consultant for Herefordshire. Brian has long experience of working both in special and mainstream schools as a teacher of mathematics. He has a range of management experience, including SENCO, mathematics and ICT co-ordinator.

Design and technology

Louise T. Davies is Principal Officer for Design and Technology at the Qualifications and Curriculum Authority and also a freelance consultant. She is an experienced presenter and author of award-winning resources and books for schools. She chairs the Special Needs Advisory Group for the Design and Technology Association.

Religious education

Dilwyn Hunt has worked as a specialist RE adviser, first in Birmingham and now in Dudley. He has a wide range of experience in the teaching of RE, including mainstream and special RE.

Music

Victoria Jaquiss is SEN specialist for music with children with emotional and behavioural difficulties in Leeds. She devised a system of musical notation primarily for use with steel pans, for which, in 2002, she was awarded the fellowship of the Royal Society of Arts.

Diane Paterson works as an inclusive music curriculum teacher in Leeds.

Geography

Diane Swift is a project leader for the Geographical Association. Her interest in special needs developed whilst she was a Staffordshire geography adviser and inspector.

PE and sport

Crispin Andrews is an education/sports writer with nine years' experience of teaching and sports coaching.

Art

Kim Earle is Able Pupils Consultant for St Helens and has been a Head of Art and Design. Kim is also a practising designer jeweller.

Gill Curry is Gifted and Talented Strand Co-ordinator for the Wirral. She has twenty years' experience as Head of Art and has also been an art advisory teacher. She is also a practising artist specialising in print.

ICT

Mike North works for ICTC, an independent consultancy specialising in the effective use of ICT in education. He develops educational materials and provides advice and support for the SEN sector.

Sally McKeown is an Education Officer with Becta, the government funded agency responsible for managing the National Grid for Learning and the FERL website. She is responsible for the use of IT for learners with disabilities, learning difficulties or additional needs.

Contents of the CD

The CD contains activities and record sheets which can be amended/ individualised and printed out for use by the purchasing institution.

Increasing the font size and spacing will improve accessibility for some students, as will changes in background colour. Alternatively, print onto pastel-coloured paper for greater ease of reading.

Legislation
The Code of Practice for Special Educational Needs
Special Educational Needs and Disability Act 2001

Special Educational Needs
Bovair's list of positive reasons and counter-arguments for all pupils to learn a language
Table 2.1 The Four Areas of Special Educational Needs
Table 4.1 Some Pupil Behaviours
Table 5.1 Left and Right Brain Learning Styles

Teaching
List of points of basic good practice
A useful model lesson structure
Good practice guide

Materials
Table 4.2 Creating Handouts
A checklist for evaluating materials
Support from technology

Administration and planning
Useful headings when establishing a working policy
P levels
Assisting with classroom resources and records

Appendices
1   Issues for MFL and SEN
2.1 MFL: Draft Policy for SEN
2.2 SEN and Disability Act 2001 (SENDA)
2.3 INSET Activity A
2.4 INSET Activity B
3   Case Studies
4.1 Whiteboards

Introduction

All teaching and non teaching staff should be involved in the development of the school's SEN policy and be fully aware of the school's procedure for identifying, assessing and making provision for pupils with SEN.

(Table of Roles and Responsibilities, Code of Practice 2002)

The revised regulations for special educational needs (SEN) provision make it clear that mainstream schools are expected to provide for pupils with a wide diversity of needs. Just a few years ago, it was rare to come across children with such conditions as cystic fibrosis or haemophilia or significant learning disabilities in mainstream schools. Now, they are entering secondary schools in growing numbers and their 'inclusion' cannot be simply the responsibility of the special needs co-ordinator (SENCO) and support staff. Teachers of all subjects have to be aware of pupils' learning needs and develop strategies in the classroom (and library, computer room or on outside visits) that directly address those requirements.

This book looks at ways of developing provision for the widest possible range of pupils in the mainstream modern foreign languages (MFL) classroom. There are examples of work in French, German and Spanish throughout the text and in the appendices. These are purely illustrative of types of activities and ways of working, and are not intended to imply that these are the only languages taught in schools today or are the only languages suitable for pupils with special needs.

Meeting Special Needs in Modern Foreign Languages does not assume that teachers are specialists either in teaching a language or in working with pupils with SEN. The book and CD are a resource that, it is hoped, will give staff confidence to contribute to departmental policy and to develop a more inclusive classroom where language learning can flourish.

CHAPTER 1

Meeting Special Educational Needs – Your Responsibility

There is no doubt that the number of children with special educational needs (SEN) being educated in mainstream schools is growing:

> . . . because of the increased emphasis on the inclusion of children with SEN in mainstream schools the number of these children is increasing, as are the severity and variety of their SEN. Children with a far wider range of learning difficulties and variety of medical conditions, as well as sensory difficulties and physical disabilities, are now attending mainstream classes. The implication of this is that mainstream school teachers need to expand their knowledge and skills with regard to the needs of children with SEN. (Stakes and Hornby 2000[1])

For teachers of modern foreign languages, the world of special needs is a labyrinth: there is so much jargon, and the descriptions of particular types of disability or syndromes seem to bear little relation to the children in their classrooms. This chapter will give you an overview of the terminology, acronyms and legislation.

What does SEN mean?

The definition which is most commonly adopted is taken from Part 1 of the Disability Discrimination Act (DDA) 1995.[2] Under the DDA, a person is considered disabled if they have 'a physical or mental impairment which has an effect on their normal day to day activities.' That effect must be:

- substantial (more than minor or trivial)
- long-term (lasting for at least 12 months)
- adverse

'Physical or mental impairments' include:

- sensory impairments

- hidden impairments (e.g. dyslexia, learning difficulties, epilepsy, diabetes, etc.)

- 'clinically well-recognised' mental illness

Progressive conditions such as MS (multiple sclerosis), cancer and HIV are covered from when the condition leads to an impairment which has some effect on the ability to carry out normal day-to-day activities.

Of course, these categories do not necessarily equate in teachers' minds with individual children they meet each day in the classroom. You will hear staff describe a pupil as 'childish' or 'totally thick' or 'in the remedial group'. These terms are inaccurate and just put a label on a child, without beginning to analyse what that child needs in the way of educational provision. Other, apparently more measured, terms can be particularly misleading. Teachers will describe a child as being 'dyslexic' when they mean that he is poor at reading and writing. 'ADHD' has become a synonym for badly behaved, while a child who seems to be withdrawn or behaves oddly is sometimes described as being 'autistic'.

The whole process of applying labels is fraught with danger. The special need becomes the focus of attention and the needs of the individual child are lost. All too easily, the attitude can become: 'He's dyslexic so he'll have problems with writing words in French so we need to set him lots of look-cover-write and check activities.' No one, however, learns a language by writing out single words out of context.

It is a fine balancing act to pay heed to the particular issues and barriers which arise from a special need and to know the child as an individual. Teachers have not only to identify the child's strengths and weaknesses but also to create a valid place for that child in a class of 20–30 children who all have their own particular requirements. Still, nobody said teaching was easy!

The Code of Practice for SEN

The 'Fundamental Principles' in the *Special Needs Code of Practice* [3] provide a clear explanation of why a school needs to examine its inclusion policies:

- A child with special educational needs should have their needs met.

- The special educational needs of children will normally be met in mainstream schools or settings.

- The views of the child should be sought and taken into account.

- Parents have a vital role to play in supporting their child's education.

- Children with special educational needs should be offered full access to a broad, balanced and relevant education, including an appropriate curriculum for the Foundation stage and the National Curriculum.

Many secondary schools have still not taken in the full implications of the legislation which amended the Code of Practice from September 2002. Its main aim is to ensure that disabled children receive equal treatment. They must not be placed at a 'substantial disadvantage' in relation to admissions or 'education and associated services'. In practical terms, this puts the pressure on schools to draw up a plan for improving both physical and cognitive access, and for LEAs to develop an accessibility strategy.

The Code of Practice (CoP) is not a statutory obligation, but schools are expected to follow it and Ofsted inspectors report on it. Pupils with significant needs will often (but not always) have a statement of special educational needs. This is a legally binding undertaking by the LEA to provide a certain amount of support in a specified way.

The CoP was revised in January 2002, to cut down on paperwork and simplify the whole process into three overlapping stages:

- **School Action**

A problem or difficulty is identified and the SENCO, in collaboration with teacher/teachers, attempts to provide additional support for a pupil.

- **School Action Plus**

If a pupil's progress is unsatisfactory, professional help is brought in, perhaps from the Learning Support Service, a specialist teacher or therapist, or an educational psychologist. An Individual Education Plan (IEP) will be introduced.

- **Referral for statutory assessment**

If, after a period of time, and appropriate interventions, there is still cause for concern, a formal, multi-disciplinary assessment can be requested, and this may lead to a statement of special educational needs.

The word 'statement' is often bandied around staffrooms, but there are many mainstream teachers who have only a vague notion as to what it is. In effect, a statement is a legal contract which outlines clearly the additional help a pupil needs, together with detail about how and when it will be delivered. Medical, psychological and educational professionals are involved in drawing up the statement, which deals with pupils who have 'severe or complex needs', and the LEA is responsible for its creation and cost. A parent, or the Head Teacher, can request a formal assessment of a child's needs, and the LEA has six weeks to respond. Parents have the right of appeal if the LEA turns them down.

What does the Act cover?

Part 4 of the Special Educational Needs and Disability Act 2001[4] was implemented from September 2002 and becomes Part 4 of the Disability Discrimination Act. The Act covers pre- and post-16 education.

The Act introduces the right for disabled pupils not be discriminated against in education, training and any services provided wholly or mainly for students or those enrolled on a course when this is provided by certain 'responsible bodies' such as schools, colleges or LEAs. This means that the Act covers not only education but other areas as well. 'Services' might include:

- arranging study abroad or work placements

- careers advice and training

- chaplaincy and prayer areas

- learning equipment and materials such as laboratory equipment, computer facilities, class handouts, etc.

- learning facilities such as classrooms, lecture theatres, laboratories, studios, darkrooms, etc.

- outings and trips

- placement finding services

- libraries, learning centres and information centres and their resources

- counselling services

- examinations and assessments

- field trips

- informal/optional study skills sessions

- information and communication technology and resources

From 1 September 2003, responsible bodies are also required to make adjustments that involve the provision of auxiliary aids and services, and after 1 September 2005, responsible bodies are required to make adjustments to the physical features of premises where these put disabled people or students at a substantial disadvantage. Of course, some of the services covered by this new Act were previously covered by Part III of the DDA 1995 but will now come under the new Act as Part IV of the DDA and will be more strictly enforced.

One of the key areas for schools to consider is that they must take steps to prevent disadvantage occurring. The duty to make 'reasonable adjustments' is a duty to disabled people generally and not just to particular individuals. This 'anticipatory' aspect effectively means that providers must consider what sort of adjustments may be necessary for disabled people in the future and, where appropriate, make adjustments in advance. These might include:

- changes to policies and practices

- changes to course requirements

- changes to the physical features of a building

- provision of interpreters or other support workers

- the delivery of courses in alternative ways

- the provision of materials in other formats

If all the staff in the MFL department produce all their materials in electronic form to ensure that they can easily be converted into large print or put into other alternative formats, such as Braille, then the staff are anticipating 'reasonable adjustments' that might need to be made.

The SENCO

Since 1992, the Audit Commission has measured an increase from 40 to 55 per cent of statemented children educated in mainstream classrooms. At the same time, the principle of inclusion has gained ground and, as a result, special schools continue to close. In recent years, the role of the special educational needs co-ordinator has grown dramatically. They may deal with as many as one in four of the children in a school and have responsibility for:

- ensuring liaison with parents and other professionals;

- advising and supporting other practitioners in the setting;

- ensuring that appropriate Individual Education Plans are in place and that relevant background information about individual children with special educational needs is collected, recorded and updated;

- making plans for future support and setting targets for improvement;

- monitoring and reviewing action taken;

- ensuring records are kept at each stage of the process;

- informing the parents of action to be taken to help the child.

Additionally, the SENCO should take the lead in further assessment of the child's particular strengths and weaknesses, in planning future support for the child in discussion with colleagues, and in monitoring and subsequently reviewing the action taken.

Inclusive schools

Teachers are there to teach, but what does this mean? No longer do staff just teach a subject: they teach children and work in diverse settings. The *Index for Inclusion* urges us all to take a fresh look at how we work and indeed, how we think. The basis of the *Index* is to create a new language whereby the concept of 'special educational needs' is replaced by the term 'barriers to learning and participation'. Consequently, the lowering of these barriers and the creation of the resources to support this is what inclusive education is about. In real terms, this represents a shift from a medical model of difficulties in education to a social one. There may be little that schools can do to overcome impairments, the *Index* argues, but they can have an impact on reducing disabilities due to physical, personal and institutional barriers to access and participation. The *Index* states that: 'Inclusion in education involves the process of increasing the participation of students in, and reducing their exclusion from, the cultures, curricula and communities of local schools.'[5]

This chimes well with the views of the DfES. On the Standards site, the Key Stage 3 National Strategy urges schools to develop a set of values and create a school ethos: 'All schools will want to attach particular importance to promoting mutual respect and understanding of different religions, cultural traditions and languages.'[6]

This set of values has permeated the curriculum in recent years with Commonwealth Literature texts set for GCSE, the legacy of Britain's colonial past studied in history and EC projects at all levels to develop a sense of the diversity of Europe. Citizenship became a statutory subject in secondary schools in September 2002 and includes legal and human rights and responsibilities, the diversity of identities in the UK, and the world as a global community.

Improving access

If we look at the guidance for teaching citizenship to pupils with special needs, it can help to shape our thinking about what we need to do in MFL and how to do it:

Staff can make PSHE and citizenship more accessible by focusing on the senses. They can improve access by:

- using materials and resources that pupils can understand through sight, touch, sound, taste or smell;
- organising a range of activities to compensate for a lack of first-hand experiences;
- giving first-hand and direct experiences through play, visits, drama, puppets.

Staff can also improve access by:

- using ICT, visual and other materials to increase pupils' knowledge of their personal surroundings and the wider world, for example, through stories;
- using specialist aids and equipment, adapting tasks or environments, or providing alternative activities, where necessary;
- encouraging support from adults or other pupils, while giving pupils space and freedom to do things for themselves and allowing time to respond. Pupils with learning difficulties are often dependent on the consistent and sensitive responses and support of staff to ensure proper access to learning opportunities;

- being aware of the pace at which pupils work and of the physical effort required;
- balancing consistency and challenge, according to individual needs;
- giving opportunities to make choices and have control in all activities.

Teaching PSHE and citizenship can help pupils develop their broader communication and literacy skills through encouraging interaction with other pupils as well as staff. With some pupils, communication and literacy skills will develop as they use a range of visual, written and tactile materials, for example large print, symbols and symbol text. These skills also develop as pupils use ICT and other technological aids. Other pupils' skills develop as they use alternative and augmentative communication, for example body movements, eye gaze, facial expressions and gestures including pointing and signing.[7]

Disapplying pupils

But while this guidance is useful, it still does not solve the dilemma facing MFL teachers in many schools: should pupils with special needs be learning another language? While all but the most xenophobic would see that it is essential to break down the barriers and make pupils aware of other worlds and cultures, opinions are divided about teaching MFL to pupils with special needs. As a contributor to Senco-forum expressed it:

> What's the point of shoving French and German down the throats of kids who are brilliant with their hands and have good DT skills when they have not yet mastered basic sentence construction or spelling/reading in English?

An activity focusing on these issues can be found in Appendix 1.

Parents also worry and think that if a child is a poor reader, then they should be receiving remedial literacy support. MFL is somehow seen as a luxury, rather then as an essential ingredient for modern living. There is an underlying assumption that clever people do languages and that a second language will be too much for a child with special educational needs, that French will get in the way of phonics or that languages and literacy will conflict.

Keith Bovair, past president of NASEN, warns of some of the changing perspectives in teaching MFL:

> I speak very little French or German or Spanish. My own education was that of an inner city young person who looked forward to continuing his part-time job at a clothing warehouse, with it turning into a full-time position. Life events unfolded and I found myself travelling the world, desiring to learn and know more, with a great desire to connect. This desire has focused my development and led to opening greater educational opportunities for others; opportunities I was denied or discouraged from because I was in the 'vocational' track. This vocational track is now on the horizon and the

exclusion of MFL at specific key stages a possible reality. This smacks of the old 'What these children need . . .' which is reminder to me of an early observation I made in regards to teaching children with special needs a foreign language. The only 'disabling' conditions that our pupils have are the low expectations and assumptions made by adults.[8]

There is also the question of league tables. If pupils cannot fulfil all the four components of listening, speaking, reading and writing, they will not achieve high grades, and this might have an effect on the school's position in the league tables. Hence, increasing numbers of pupils on the SEN register are 'disapplied', and will end up with fewer language skills than their peers.

There are so many arguments to contend with, but here is a typical selection of justifications for excluding children with special needs from the modern foreign languages classroom.

It's not a core subject like science. Megan has had so much time off with her operations, she would be better off dropping languages and concentrating on the core subjects.

Kuli is deaf. He can't hear, so how can he ever learn a language?

Steven isn't coping well with school. He's in danger of being suspended. We need to make sure he isn't under too much pressure or he could blow.

Bhavini can't see very well. All her English spelling is phonic. Spanish would make things worse. She's better off having extra English support.

Matthew has learning difficulties. It takes him all his time to get to class and listen. He certainly won't follow a foreign language.

Susan has the attention span of a goldfish. She won't pass an exam. She won't stop talking long enough to let you get a word in edgeways – in either language!

Jenny has done well to stay in mainstream but now she'll start falling behind the other children. It's better that she concentrates on things she's good at. She can join in with the other children for most of the classes but German would be a bit much.

Harry is dyslexic. Learning French will just make his spelling worse.

But there are all sorts of positive reasons and counter-arguments for all pupils to learn a language. Bovair argues that the MFL curriculum is an ideal vehicle:

- to develop pupils' self-esteem;

- to provide intellectual stimulation and to promote skills of more general application;

- to develop pupils' ability to communicate in another language;

- to develop general language skills through a new learning experience leading to a positive achievement;

- to develop pupils' capabilities in their own language;

- to learn about the countries where the target languages are spoken, and to encourage positive attitudes towards different cultures;

- to ensure all pupils achieve a degree of understanding that their village, town or city and the UK are all part of the European Union;

- to give pupils the opportunity to appreciate similarities and differences in lifestyles and customs and to learn that differences and diversity are an asset rather than a threat to living as a community;

- to establish links with other European countries;

- to appreciate the implications for everyday living of the European market.[9]

Pupils with a wide range of needs – physical, emotional, cognitive and social – are to be found in every classroom in Britain. Learning a foreign language is a challenge but it is also a significant factor in helping children to appreciate the different communities and cultures in the modern world. Government policies only point the way. Teachers are ultimately responsible for the children whom they teach; it is up to teachers to make the rhetoric a reality.

Notes

1 Stakes, R. and Hornby, G. (2000) *Meeting Special Needs in Mainstream Schools: A Practical Guide for Teachers*, 3. London: David Fulton Publishers.
2 Disability Discrimination Act 1995 (c.50) The Stationery Office Limited.
3 DfES (revised 2002) *Special Needs Code of Practice*, www.dfes.gov.uk/sen/
4 Special Educational Needs and Disability Act 2001, HMSO: http://www.hmso.gov.uk
5 Booth, T. and Ainscow, M. (2000) *The Index for Inclusion*, Centre for Studies on Inclusive Education, New Redland, Frenchay Campus, Coldharbour Lane, Bristol BS16 1QU Tel: +44 117 344 4007 Fax: +44 117 344 4005.
6 DfES (2002) Key Stage 3 National Strategy: *Designing the Key Stage 3 Curriculum*, DfES 2002. Obtainable from: www.standards.dfes.gov.uk/midbins/keystage3/DKS3Camended.pdf
7 'Responding to pupils' needs when teaching PSHE and citizenship': http://www.nc.uk.net/ld/PSHE_respond.html
8 Bovair, K. (2002) *MFL*, CILT's bulletin for secondary language teachers, Autumn 2002, 7.
9 Op. cit. Bovair, K. CILT.

CHAPTER 2

Departmental Policy

Every department needs a policy that outlines strategies for meeting pupils' special educational needs. The policy should set the scene for any visitor to the MFL department – from supply staff to inspectors – and make a valuable contribution to the departmental handbook. The process of developing a department SEN policy offers the opportunity to clarify and evaluate current thinking and practice within the MFL team and to establish a consistent approach.

The policy should:

- clarify the responsibilities of all staff and identify any with specialist training and/or knowledge;

- describe the curriculum on offer and how it can be differentiated;

- outline arrangements for assessment and reporting;

- guide staff on how to work effectively with support staff;

- identify staff training.

The starting point will be the school's SEN policy as required by the Education Act 1996, with each subject department 'fleshing out' the detail in a way which describes how things work in practice. The writing of a policy should be much more than a paper exercise completed to satisfy the senior management team and Ofsted inspectors: it is an opportunity for staff to come together as a team and create a framework for teaching languages in a way that makes them accessible to all pupils in the school. (See Appendix 1, INSET activity.)

Where to start when writing a policy

An audit can act as a starting point for reviewing current policy on SEN or to inform the writing of a new policy. It will involve gathering information and reviewing current practice with regard to pupils with SEN and is best completed by the whole of the department, preferably with some additional advice from the SENCO or another member of staff with responsibility for SEN within the school. An audit carried out by the whole department can provide a valuable opportunity for professional development if it is seen as an exercise in sharing good practice and encouraging joint planning. But before embarking on an audit, it is worth investing some time in a department meeting or training day. With the best will in the world, it is all too easy for meetings to become a series of grumbles punctuated by 'They can't . . .' statements. One tip learned from visits to the United States is to make everyone start with: 'One thing that I've found that works is . . .'

In fact, we learn much more from our successes than from our failures. If we find a strategy that works, we can analyse it and extrapolate from it and apply it to other sets of circumstances. In our constant attempts to analyse our failures we are always in the dark. No one knows precisely why a scheme or particular ploy doesn't work. There may be a whole host of reasons. But when we look at our successes, that's a different story altogether. Successes may be small but significant:

'Stephen can concentrate if he is sitting at the front of the class.'

'Now I've learnt to finger spell, Kuli seems to remember more words and can write them down.'

'The sponsored German bee really motivated 7J to learn their vocabulary.'

Useful headings when establishing a working policy

General statement

- What does legislation and DfES guidance say?

- What does the school policy state?

- What do members of the department have to do to comply with it?

Definition of SEN

- What does SEN mean?

- What are the areas of need and the categories used in the Code of Practice?

- Are there any special implications within the subject area?

Provision for staff within the department

- Who has responsibility for SEN within the department?

- How and when is information shared?

- Where and what information is stored?

Provision for pupils with SEN

- How are pupils with SEN assessed and monitored in the department?

- How are contributions to IEPs and reviews made?

- What criteria are used for organising teaching groups?

- What alternative courses are offered to pupils with SEN?

- What special internal and external examination arrangements are made?

- What guidance is available for working with support staff?

Resources and learning materials

- Is there any specialist equipment used in the department?

- How are resources developed?

- Where are resources stored?

Staff qualifications and Continuing Professional Development needs

- What qualifications do the members of the department have?

- What training has taken place?

- How is training planned?

- Is a record kept of training completed and training needs?

Monitoring and reviewing the policy

- How will the policy be monitored?

- When will the policy be reviewed?

The content of an SEN departmental policy

This section gives detailed information on what an SEN policy might include. Each heading is expanded with some detailed information and raises the main issues with regard to teaching pupils with SEN. At the end of each section there is a sample statement. These can be personalised and brought together to make a policy. A sample policy can be found in Appendix 2.

General statement with reference to the school's SEN policy

All schools must have an SEN policy according to the Education Act 1996. This policy will set out basic information on the school's SEN provision, how the school identifies, assesses and provides for pupils with SEN, including information on staffing and working in partnership with other professionals and parents.

Any department policy needs to have reference to the school SEN policy.

Example

> All members of the department will ensure that the needs of all pupils with SEN are met, according to the aims of the school and its SEN policy.

Definition of SEN

It is useful to insert at least the four areas of SEN in the department policy, as used in the Code of Practice for Special Educational Needs.

TABLE 2.1 THE FOUR AREAS OF SEN

Cognition and Learning Needs	Behavioural, Emotional and Social Development Needs	Communication and Interaction Needs	Sensory and/or Physical Needs
Specific learning difficulties (SpLD)	Behavioural, emotional and social difficulties (BESD)	Speech, language and communication needs	Hearing impairment (HI)
Dyslexia			Visual impairment (VI)
		Autistic Spectrum Disorder (ASD)	
Moderate learning difficulties (MLD)	Attention Deficit Disorder (ADD)		Multi-sensory impairment (MSI)
		Asperger's Syndrome	
Severe learning difficulties (SLD)	Attention Deficit Hyperactivity Disorder (ADHD)		Physical difficulties (PD)
Profound and multiple learning difficulties (PMLD)			OTHER

Provision for staff within the department

In many schools, each department nominates a member of staff to have special responsibility for SEN provision (with or without remuneration). This can be very effective where there is a system of regular liaison between department SEN representatives and the SENCO in the form of meetings or paper communications or a mixture of both.

The responsibilities of this post may include liaison between the department and the SENCO, attending any liaison meetings and providing feedback via meetings and minutes, attending training, maintaining the departmental SEN information and records and representing the needs of pupils with SEN at departmental level. This post can be seen as a valuable development opportunity for staff. The name of this person should be included in the policy.

How members of the department raise concerns about pupils with SEN can be included in this section. Concerns may be raised at specified departmental meetings before referral to the SENCO. An identified member of the department could make referrals to the SENCO and keep a record of this information.

Reference to working with support staff will include a commitment to planning and communication between staff. There may be information on inviting support staff to meetings, resources and lesson plans.

A reference to the centrally held lists of pupils with SEN and other relevant information will also be included in this section. A note about confidentiality of information should be included.

Example

> The member of staff with responsibility for overseeing the provision of SEN within the department will attend liaison meetings and feed back to other members of the department. He will maintain the department's SEN information file, attend appropriate training and disseminate this to all departmental staff. All information will be treated with confidentiality.

Provision for pupils with SEN

It is the responsibility of all staff to know which pupils have SEN and to identify any pupils having difficulties. Pupils with SEN may be identified by staff within the department in a variety of ways, which may be listed and could include:

- observation in lessons

- assessment of class work

- homework tasks

- end of module tests

- progress checks

- annual examinations

- reports

Setting out how pupils with SEN are grouped within the MFL department may include specifying the criteria used and/or the philosophy behind the method of grouping.

Example

The pupils are grouped according to ability as informed by Key Stage 2 results, reading scores and any other relevant performance, social or medical information.

Monitoring arrangements and details of how pupils can move between groups should also be set out. Information collected may include:

- National Curriculum levels

- departmental assessments

- reading scores

- advice from pastoral staff

- discussion with staff in the SEN department

- information provided on IEPs

Special examination arrangements need to be considered not only at Key Stages 3 and 4 but also for internal examinations. How and when these will be discussed should be clarified. Reference to SENCO and examination arrangements from the examination board should be taken into account. Ensuring that staff in the department understand the current legislation and guidance from central government is important, so a reference to the SEN Code of Practice and the levels of SEN intervention is helpful within the policy. Here is a good place also to put a statement about the school behaviour policy and rewards and sanctions, and how the department will make any necessary adjustments to meet the needs of pupils with SEN.

Example

It is understood that pupils with SEN may receive additional support if they have a statement of SEN, are at School Action Plus or School Action. The staff in the MFL department will aim to support the pupils to achieve their targets as specified on their IEPs and will provide feedback for IEP or statement reviews. Pupils with SEN will be included in the departmental monitoring system used for all pupils. Additional support will be requested as appropriate.

Resources and learning materials

The department policy needs to specify what differentiated materials are available, where they are kept and how to find new resources. This section could include a statement about working with support staff to develop resources or access specialist resources as needed, and the use of ICT.

Teaching strategies may also be identified if appropriate. Advice on more specialist equipment can be sought as necessary, possibly through LEA support services: contact details may be available from the SENCO, or the department may have direct links. Any specially bought subject text or alternative/ appropriate courses can be specified as well as any external assessment and examination courses.

Example

> The department will provide suitably differentiated materials and, where appropriate, specialist resources for pupils with SEN. Additional texts are available for those pupils working below National Curriculum level 3. At Key Stage 4 an alternative course to GCSE is offered at Entry level but, where possible, pupils with SEN will be encouraged to reach their full potential and follow a GCSE course. Support staff will be provided with curriculum information in advance of lessons and will also be involved in lesson planning. A list of resources is available in the department handbook and on the noticeboard.

ICT

When looking at resources, make sure staff consider ICT provision as well as books and taped resources. Many schools have access to framework software such as *Clicker* or *Writing with Symbols* but never consider how useful it can be for differentiating the curriculum in French or German. Also, as so many pupils are not so much slow learners as 'quick forgetters', the MFL department needs a policy on revision and consolidation.

Staff qualifications and Continuing Professional Development needs

It is important to recognise and record the qualifications and special skills gained by staff within the department. Training can include not only external courses but also in-house INSET and opportunities such as observing other staff, working to produce materials with other staff, and visiting other establishments. Staff may have hidden skills that might enhance the work of the department and the school: for example, some staff might be proficient in the use of sign language; some TAs may have undertaken a specialist qualification in dyslexia while others may have excellent computer skills. CILT offers Comenius funded residential language courses as well as NOF training for ICT in the MFL classroom.

Example

> A record of training undertaken, specialist skills and training required will be kept in the department handbook. Requests for training will be considered in line with the department and school improvement plan.

Monitoring and reviewing the policy

To be effective any policy needs regular monitoring and review. These can be planned as part of the yearly cycle. The responsibility for the monitoring can rest with the Head of Department but will have more effect if supported by someone from outside acting as a critical friend. This could be the SENCO or a member of the senior management team in school.

Example

> The department SEN policy will be monitored by the Head of Department on a planned annual basis, with advice being sought from the SENCO as part of a three-yearly review process.

Summary

Creating a departmental SEN policy should be a developmental activity to improve the teaching and learning for all pupils but especially those with special or additional needs. The policy should be a working document that will evolve and change; it is there to challenge current practice and to encourage improvement for both pupils and staff. If departmental staff work together to create the policy, they will have ownership of it; it will have true meaning and be effective in clarifying practice.

Different Types of SEN

This chapter will not turn you into an instant expert on disabilities or learning difficulties. It is a starting point for information on the special educational needs most frequently found in the mainstream secondary school. It describes the main characteristics of each learning difficulty with practical ideas for the MFL classroom, and contacts for further information. Some of the tips are based on good secondary practice while others encourage teachers to try new or less familiar approaches.

The special educational needs outlined in this chapter are grouped under the headings used in the SEN Code of Practice (DfES 2001):

- cognition and learning

- behaviour, emotional and social development

- communication and interaction

- sensory and/or physical needs

(See Table 2.1 in Chapter 2.)

The labels used in this chapter are useful when describing pupils' difficulties, but it is important to remember not to use the label in order to define the pupil. Put the pupil before the difficulty, saying 'the pupil with special educational needs' rather than 'the SEN pupil', 'pupils with moderate learning difficulties' rather than 'MLDs'.

Remember to take care in using labels when talking with parents, pupils or other professionals. Unless a pupil has a firm diagnosis, and parents and pupil understand the implications of that diagnosis, it is more appropriate to describe the features of the special educational need rather than use the label. For example, a teacher might describe a pupil's spelling difficulties but not use the term 'dyslexic'.

The number and profile of pupils with special educational needs will vary from school to school, so it is important to consider the pupil with SEN as an individual within your school and subject environment. The strategies contained in this chapter will help teachers adapt that environment to meet the needs of individual pupils within the subject context. For example, rather than saying, 'He can't read the worksheet', recognise that the worksheet is too difficult for the pupil, and adapt the work accordingly.

There is a continuum of need within each of the special educational needs listed here. Some pupils will be affected more than others, and show fewer or more of the characteristics described.

The availability and levels of support from professionals within a school (e.g. SENCOs, support teachers and Teaching Assistants (TAs)) and external professionals (e.g. educational psychologists, Learning Support Service staff and medical staff) will depend on the severity of pupils' SEN. This continuum of need will also impact on the subject teacher's planning and allocation of support staff.

Pupils with other less common special educational needs may be included in some secondary schools, and additional information on these conditions may be found in a variety of sources. These include the school SENCO, LEA support services, educational psychologists and the Internet. Appendix 3 provides more detailed case studies of eight children and some starter strategies for working in the MFL classroom.

Asperger's Syndrome

Asperger's Syndrome is a disorder at the able end of the autistic spectrum. People with Asperger's Syndrome have average to high intelligence but share the same Triad of Impairments. They often want to make friends but do not understand the complex rules of social interaction. They have impaired fine and gross motor skills, with writing being a particular problem. Boys are more likely to be affected – with the ratio being 10:1 boys to girls. Because they appear 'odd' and naïve, these pupils are particularly vulnerable to bullying.

Main characteristics:

● **Social interaction**
Pupils want friends but have not developed the strategies necessary for making and sustaining friendships. They find it very difficult to learn social norms and to pick up on social cues. Social situations, such as lessons, can cause anxiety.

● **Social communication**
Pupils have appropriate spoken language but tend to sound formal and pedantic, using little expression and with an unusual tone of voice. They have difficulty using and understanding non-verbal language, such as facial expression, gesture, body language and eye contact. They have a literal understanding of language and do not grasp implied meanings.

● **Social imagination**
Pupils with Asperger's Syndrome need structured environments, and to have routines they understand and can anticipate. They excel at learning facts and figures, but have difficulty understanding abstract concepts and in generalising information and skills. They often have all-consuming special interests.

How can the MFL teacher help?

● Create as calm a classroom environment as possible.
● Allow the pupil to sit in the same place for each lesson.
● Set up a work buddy system for your lessons.
● Provide additional visual cues in class (realia such as menus).
● Give time to process questions and respond.
● Check pupils understand what to do. Ask them to repeat back instructions.
● Allow alternatives to writing for recording. Use tapes/drawings.
● Use visual timetables and task activity lists.
● Prepare for changes to routines well in advance.

The National Autistic Society, 393 City Road, London ECIV 1NG
Tel: 0845 070 4004 Helpline (10a.m. – 4p.m., Mon–Fri)
Tel: 020 7833 2299 Fax: 020 7833 9666
Email: nas@nas.org.uk Website: http://www.nas.org.uk

Attention Deficit Disorder (with or without hyperactivity) (ADD/ADHD)

Attention Deficit Hyperactivity Disorder is a term used to describe children who are over-active or exceptionally impulsive, and who have difficulty in paying attention. It is caused by a form of brain dysfunction of a genetic nature. ADHD can sometimes be controlled effectively by medication. Children of all levels of ability can have ADHD.

Main characteristics:

- difficulty in following instructions and completing tasks
- easily distracted by noise, movement of others, objects attracting attention
- often doesn't listen when spoken to
- fidgets and becomes restless, can't sit still
- interferes with other pupils' work
- can't stop talking, interrupts others, calls out
- runs about when inappropriate
- has difficulty in waiting or taking turns
- acts impulsively without thinking about the consequences

How can the MFL teacher help?

- Make eye contact and use the pupil's name when speaking to him.
- Keep instructions simple.
- Provide clear routines and rules and rehearse them regularly.
- Sit the pupil away from obvious distractions, e.g. windows.
- In busy situations direct the pupil by name to visual or practical objects.
- Encourage the pupil to repeat back instructions before starting work.
- Tell the pupil when to start a task.
- Give two choices – avoid the option of the pupil saying 'No' by asking, 'Do you want to write in blue or black pen?'
- Give advanced warning when something is about to happen. Change or finish with a time, e.g. 'Paul, in two minutes I need you to get your dictionary out . . .'
- Give specific praise – catch him being good, give attention for positive behaviour.
- Give the pupil responsibilities so that others can see him in a positive light and he develops a positive self-image.

ADD Information Services, PO Box 340, Edgware, Middlesex HA8 9HL
Tel: 020 8906 9068
ADDNET UK Website: www.btinternet.com/~black.ice/addnet/

Autistic Spectrum Disorders (ASD)

The term 'Autistic Spectrum Disorders' is used for a range of disorders affecting the development of social interaction, social communication and social imagination and flexibility of thought. This is known as the 'Triad of Impairments'. Pupils with ASD cover the full range of ability, and the severity of the impairment varies widely. Some pupils also have learning disabilities or other difficulties. Four times as many boys as girls are diagnosed with an ASD.

Main characteristics:

- **Social interaction**
  Pupils with an ASD find it difficult to understand social behaviour and this affects their ability to interact with children and adults. They do not always understand social contexts. They may experience high levels of stress and anxiety in settings that do not meet their needs or when routines are changed. This can lead to inappropriate behaviour.

- **Social communication**
  Understanding and use of non-verbal and verbal communication is impaired. Pupils with an ASD have difficulty understanding others and in developing effective communication themselves. They have a literal understanding of language. Many are delayed in learning to speak, and some never develop speech at all.

- **Social imagination and flexibility of thought**
  Pupils with an ASD have difficulty in thinking and behaving flexibly which may result in restricted, obsessional, or repetitive activities. They are often more interested in objects than people, and may have intense interests in one particular area, such as trains or horses. Pupils work best when they have a routine. Unexpected changes in those routines will cause distress. Some pupils with Autistic Spectrum Disorders have a different perception of sounds, sights, smell, touch, and taste, and this can affect their response to these sensations.

How can subject teachers help?

- Liaise with parents as they will have many useful strategies.
- Provide visual supports in class: objects, pictures, picture dictionaries.
- Give advance warning of any changes to usual routines.
- Provide either an individual desk or with a work buddy.
- Avoid using too much eye contact as it can cause distress.
- Give individual instructions using the pupil's name, 'Paul, bring me your book.'
- Use computers. There are many MFL packages where learners can practise dialogues with an on-screen partner. This may be less stressful than working with another pupil.
- Develop social interactions using a buddy system or Circle of Friends.
- Avoid using metaphor, idiom or sarcasm – say what you mean in simple terms.
- Teach some vocabulary which relates to special interests, e.g. train vocabulary.

BEHAVIOURAL, EMOTIONAL AND SOCIAL DEVELOPMENT NEEDS

This term includes behavioural, emotional and social difficulties and Attention Deficit Disorder with or without hyperactivity. These difficulties can be seen across the whole ability range and have a continuum of severity. Pupils with special educational needs in this category are those who have persistent difficulties despite an effective school behaviour policy and a personal and social curriculum.

Behavioural, emotional, social difficulty (BESD)

Main characteristics:

- inattentive, poor concentration and lack of interest in school/school work
- easily frustrated, anxious about changes
- unable to work in groups
- unable to work independently, constantly seeking help
- confrontational – verbally aggressive towards pupils and/or adults
- physically aggressive towards pupils and/or adults
- destroys property – their own/others
- appears withdrawn, distressed, unhappy, sulky, may self-harm
- lacks confidence, may appear to be extremely frightened, lacks self-esteem
- finds it difficult to communicate
- finds it difficult to accept praise

How can the MFL teacher help?

- Talk to the pupil to find out a bit about them. As language learning involves a lot of personal information, check what they are happy to disclose. Not every pupil is willing to discuss family and home.
- Check the ability level of the pupil and adapt the level of work to this.
- Consider the pupil's strengths and use them.
- Tell the pupil what you expect in advance, as regards work and behaviour.
- Set a subject target with a reward system.
- Focus your comments on the behaviour not on the pupil and offer an alternative way of behaving when correcting the pupil.
- Use positive language and verbal praise whenever possible.
- Tell the pupil what you want them to do: 'I need you to . . .', 'I want you to . . .' rather than ask. This avoids confrontation and allows the possibility that there is room for negotiation.
- Give the pupil a choice between two options.
- Be consistent. Stick to what you say and do not negotiate as this breeds insecurity.
- Involve the pupil in responsibilities to increase self-esteem and confidence.
- Plan a 'time out' system. Ask a colleague for help with this.

SEBDA is the new name for the Association of Workers for Children with Emotional and Behavioural Difficulties.
Website: http://www.awcebd.co.uk

Cerebral palsy (CP)

Cerebral palsy is a persistent disorder of movement and posture. It is caused by damage or lack of development to part of the brain before or during birth or in early childhood. Problems vary from slight clumsiness to more severe lack of control of movements. Pupils with CP may also have learning difficulties. They may use a wheelchair or other mobility aid.

Main characteristics:

There are three main forms of cerebral palsy:

- **spasticity** – disordered control of movement associated with stiffened muscles

- **athetosis** – frequent involuntary movements

- **ataxia** – an unsteady gait with balance difficulties and poor spatial awareness

    Pupils may also have communication difficulties.

How can the MFL teacher help?

- Talk to parents, the physiotherapist – and the pupil.

- Consider the classroom layout.

- Have high academic expectations.

- Use visual supports: objects, pictures, symbols.

- Arrange a work/subject buddy.

- Speak directly to the pupil rather than through a TA.

- Ensure access to appropriate ICT equipment for the subject. If it is the pupil's voice, it must be set up in every session.

- Provide opportunities for practising and speaking the language in a supportive environment. Even if the pupil's speech is hard to distinguish, the practice does help to improve memory and comprehension.

- Make sure the department has a word-processing package with language characters, accents, etc.

Scope, PO Box 833, Milton Keynes, MK12 5NY
Tel: 0808 800 3333 (Freephone helpline) Fax: 01908 321051
Email: cphelpline@scope.org.uk Website: http://www.scope.org.uk

Down's Syndrome (DS)

This is a genetic condition caused by the presence of an extra chromosome 21. People with DS have varying degrees of learning difficulties ranging from mild to severe. They have a specific learning profile with characteristic strengths and weaknesses. All share certain physical characteristics but will also inherit family traits, in physical features and personality. They may have additional sight, hearing, respiratory and heart problems.

Main characteristics:

- delayed motor skills
- take longer to learn and consolidate new skills
- limited concentration
- difficulties with generalisation, thinking and reasoning
- sequencing difficulties
- stronger visual than aural skills

How can the MFL teacher help?

- Ensure that the pupil can see and hear you and other pupils.
- Speak directly to the pupil and reinforce with facial expression, pictures etc.
- Use simple, familiar language in short sentences.
- Check instructions have been understood.
- Give time for the pupil to process information and formulate a response.
- Break lessons up into a series of shorter, varied, and achievable tasks.
- Accept other ways of recording: drawings, tape/video recordings, symbols.
- Use lots of pictures, symbols and realia to reinforce language.
- Use games and fun activities.
- Set differentiated tasks linked to the work of the rest of the class.
- Provide age-appropriate resources and activities.
- Allow working in top sets to give good behaviour models.
- Provide a work buddy, but expect unsupported work for part of each lesson.

The Down's Syndrome Association, Langdon Down Centre, 2a Langdon Park, Teddington, TW11 9PS
Tel: 0845 230 0372
Email: info@downs-syndrome.org.uk
Website: http://www.downs-syndrome.org.uk

Fragile X Syndrome

Fragile X Syndrome is caused by a malformation of the X chromosome and is the most common form of inherited learning disability. This intellectual disability varies widely, with up to a third having learning problems ranging from moderate to severe. More boys than girls are affected but both may be carriers.

Main characteristics:

- delayed and disordered speech and language development
- difficulties with the social use of language
- articulation and/or fluency difficulties
- verbal skills better developed than reasoning skills
- repetitive or obsessive behaviour, such as hand-flapping, chewing, etc.
- clumsiness and fine motor co-ordination problems
- attention deficit and hyperactivity
- easily anxious or overwhelmed in busy environments.

How can the MFL teacher help?

- Make sure the pupil knows what is to happen in each lesson – provide visual timetables, work schedules or written lists.
- Ensure the pupil sits at the front of the class, preferably in the same seat for all lessons.
- Arrange a work/subject buddy.
- Where possible keep to routines and give prior warning of all changes.
- Make instructions clear and simple.
- Use visual supports: objects, pictures, symbols.
- Allow the pupil to use a computer to record and access information.
- Give lots of praise and positive feedback.
- Provide large flashcards with picture-supported vocabulary that pupils can manipulate. This will also help to focus their attention.

Fragile X Society, Rood End House, 6 Stortford Road, Dunmow, CM6 1DA
Tel: 01424 813147 (Helpline) Tel: 01371 875100 (Office)
Email: info@fragilex.org.uk Website: http://www.fragilex.org.uk

Moderate learning difficulties (MLD)

This term is used to describe pupils who find it extremely difficult to achieve expected levels of attainment across the curriculum, even with a differentiated approach. They do not find learning easy and can suffer from low self-esteem, sometimes exhibiting unacceptable behaviour as a way of avoiding failure.

Main characteristics:

- difficulties with reading, writing and comprehension
- unable to understand and retain basic mathematical skills and concepts
- immature social and emotional skills
- limited vocabulary and communication skills
- short attention span and difficulty remembering what has been taught
- under-developed co-ordination skills
- lack of logical reasoning
- inability to transfer and apply skills to different situations
- difficulty with organising themselves, following a timetable, remembering books and equipment.

How can the MFL teacher help?

- Check the pupil's strengths, weaknesses and attainment levels.
- Talk, do, check, repeat if necessary.
- Repeat information in different ways, questioning the pupil to check they have grasped a concept or can follow instructions.
- Keep tasks short and varied. Make listening tasks very brief.
- Provide word lists, writing frames, shorten text.
- Try alternative methods of recording information, e.g. drawings, charts, labelling, diagrams, use of ICT, tapes, drawings.
- Show the child what to do or what the expected outcome is, demonstrate or show examples of completed work.
- Use practical, concrete, visual examples to illustrate explanations.
- Make sure the pupil always has something to do.
- Use lots of praise, instant rewards – catch them trying hard.
- Establish a routine within the lesson.

The MLD Alliance, c/o The Elfrida Society, 34 Islington Park Street, London N1 1PX
Website: www.mldalliance.com/executive.htm

Physical disability (PD)

There is a wide range of physical disabilities, and pupils with PD cover all academic abilities. Some pupils are able to access the curriculum and learn effectively without additional educational provision. They have a disability but do not have a special educational need. For other pupils, the impact on their education may be severe, and the school will need to make adjustments to enable them to access the curriculum.

Some pupils with a physical disability have associated medical conditions which may impact on their mobility. These include cerebral palsy, heart disease, spina bifida and hydrocephalus, and muscular dystrophy. Pupils with physical disabilities may also have sensory impairments, neurological problems, or learning difficulties. They may use a wheelchair and/or additional mobility aids. Some pupils will be mobile but may have significant fine motor difficulties which require support. Others may need augmentative or alternative communication aids.

Pupils with a physical disability may need to miss lessons to attend physiotherapy or medical appointments. They are also likely to become very tired as they expend greater effort to complete everyday tasks. Schools will need to be flexible and sensitive to individual pupil needs.

How can the MFL teacher help?

- Get to know pupils and parents and they will help you make the right adjustments.

- Maintain high expectations.

- Consider the classroom layout.

- Allow the pupil to leave lessons a few minutes early to avoid busy corridors and give time to get to the next lesson.

- Set homework earlier in the lesson so instructions are not missed.

- Speak directly to the pupil rather than through a TA.

- Let pupils make their own decisions.

- Ensure access to appropriate IT equipment for the lesson – and that it is used!

- Give alternative ways of recording work.

- Plan to cover work missed through medical or physiotherapy appointments.

- Be sensitive to fatigue, especially at the end of the school day.

- Provide tapes for listening comprehension practice.

Semantic Pragmatic Disorder

Semantic Pragmatic Disorder is a communication disorder which falls within the autistic spectrum. 'Semantic' refers to the meanings of words and phrases and 'pragmatic' refers to the use of language in a social context. Pupils with this disorder have difficulties understanding the meaning of what people say and in using language to communicate effectively. Pupils with SPD find it difficult to extract the central meaning – saliency – of situations.

Main characteristics:

- delayed language development
- fluent speech but may sound stilted or over-formal
- may repeat phrases out of context from videos or adult conversations
- difficulty understanding abstract concepts
- limited or inappropriate use of eye contact, facial expression or gesture
- motor skills problems

How can the MFL teacher help?

- Sit the pupil at the front of the room to avoid distractions.
- Use visual supports: objects, pictures, symbols.
- Pair with a 'work/subject buddy'.
- Create a calm working environment with clear classroom rules.
- Be specific and unambiguous when giving instructions.
- Ensure extra practice on the contexts in which language is used.

AFASIC, 2nd Floor, 50–52 Great Sutton Street, London EC1V 0DJ
Tel: 0845 355 5577 (Helpline 11a.m. to 2p.m.)
Tel: 020 7490 9410 Fax: 020 7251 2834
Email: info@afasic.org.uk Website: http://www.afasic.org.uk

Sensory impairments

Hearing impairment (HI)

The term 'hearing impairment' is a generic term used to describe all hearing loss. The main types of loss are monaural, conductive, sensory and mixed loss. The degree of hearing loss is described as mild, moderate, severe or profound. Some children rely on lip reading, others will use hearing aids, and a small proportion will have British Sign Language (BSL) as their primary means of communication.

How can the MFL teacher help?

- Ask about the degree of hearing loss the pupil has.

- Check the best seating position (e.g. away from the hum of OHP or computers, with good ear to speaker).

- Check that the pupil can see your face for facial expressions and lip reading.

- Make sure the light falls on your face and lips. Do not stand with your back to a window.

- If you use interactive whiteboards, ensure that the beam does not prevent the pupil from seeing your face.

- Provide extra practice for lip shapes to produce the correct sounds.

- Some teachers reinforce new vocabulary by linking it with the BSL sign.

- Provide a list of vocabulary, context and visual clues.

- Provide tapes which can be used for extra practice.

- Provide transcription of oral activities.

- During class discussion allow only one pupil to speak at a time and indicate where the speaker is.

- Ban small talk!

- Establish quiet areas in the classroom.

- Check that any aids are working and whether there is any other specialist equipment available.

Royal Institute for the Deaf (RNID), 19–23 Featherstone Street, London EC1Y 8SL
Tel: 0808 808 0123
British Deaf Association (BDA) 1–3 Worship Street, London EC2A 2AB
British Association of Teachers of the Deaf (BATOD), The Orchard, Leven,
North Humberside HU17 5QA
Website: www.batod.org.uk

Visual impairment (VI)

Visual impairment refers to a range of difficulties, including those experienced by pupils with monocular vision (vision in one eye), those who are partially sighted and those who are blind. Pupils with visual impairment cover the whole ability range and some pupils may have other SEN.

How can the MFL teacher help?

- Find out the degree of sight impairment.

- Check the optimum position for the pupil, e.g. for a monocular pupil their good eye should be towards the action.

- Check that the use of interactive whiteboards does not disadvantage the child.

- If you are using video clips, explain the context. If necessary, pause the video and describe what is happening on the screen.

- Always provide the pupil with his own copy of the text.

- Provide enlarged print copies of written text.

- Check use of ICT (enlarged icons, talking text, teach keyboard skills).

- Do not stand with your back to the window as this creates a silhouette and makes it harder for the pupil to see you.

- Draw the pupil's attention to displays – which they may not notice.

- Make sure the floor is kept free of clutter.

- Tell the pupil if there is a change to the layout of a space.

- Ask if there is any specialist equipment available (enlarged print dictionaries, lights, talking scales).

- Consider using a word-processing package with a foreign language speech engine, such as *TextEase*, so that the pupil can have text read aloud.

- Look at alternative format papers for exams. The alternatives are enlarged, modified enlarged and Braille papers. You can apply for additional time for pupils. Also available is the use of technological aids and an amanuensis (scribe), reader or practical assistant to aid the pupil to gain access to, or respond to, the questions in the examination.

Royal National Institute of the Blind, 105 Judd Street, London WC1H 9NE
Tel: 020 7388 1266 Fax: 020 7388 2034 Website: http://www.rnib.org.uk

Multi-sensory impairment

Pupils with multi-sensory impairment have a combination of visual and hearing difficulties. They may also have other additional disabilities that make their situation complex. A pupil with these difficulties is likely to have a high level of individual support.

How can the MFL teacher help?

- The subject teacher will need to liaise with support staff to ascertain the appropriate provision within each subject.

- Consideration will need to be given to alternative means of communication.

- Be prepared to be flexible and to adapt tasks, targets and assessment procedures.

Severe learning difficulties (SLD)

This term covers a wide and varied group of pupils who have significant intellectual or cognitive impairments. Many have communication difficulties and/or sensory impairments in addition to more general cognitive impairments. They may also have difficulties with mobility, co-ordination and perception. Some pupils may use signs and symbols to support their communication and understanding. Their attainments may be within or below level 1 of the National Curriculum, or in the upper P scale range (P4–P8), for much of their school careers.

How can the MFL teacher help?

- Arrange a work/subject buddy.

- Use visual supports: objects, pictures, symbols.

- Learn some signs relevant to the subject.

- Allow the pupil time to process information and formulate responses.

- Set differentiated tasks linked to the work of the rest of the class.

- Set achievable targets for each lesson or module of work.

- Accept different recording methods: drawings, audio or video recordings, photographs, etc.

- Use pictures and magazines.

- Give a series of short, varied activities within each lesson.

- Use a symbol package on the computer. (*Writing with Symbols 2000* from Widgit. There are French, German and Spanish options.)

- Devise 'doing' activities which use the target language, such as cooking.

- Create stimuli which appeal to the senses – smells, things to touch and eat.

- Make it real! Invite a French/German/Spanish person into class to talk.

- Take photographs to record experiences and responses.

Profound and multiple learning difficulties (PMLD)

Pupils with profound and multiple learning difficulties (PMLD) have complex learning needs. In addition to very severe learning difficulties, pupils have other significant difficulties, such as physical disabilities, sensory impairments or severe medical conditions. Pupils with PMLD require a high level of adult support, both for their learning needs and for their personal care.

They are able to access the curriculum through sensory experiences and stimulation. Some pupils communicate by gesture, eye pointing or symbols, others by very simple language. Their attainments are likely to remain in the early P scale range (P1–P4) throughout their school careers (that is below level 1 of the National Curriculum). The P scales provide small, achievable steps to monitor progress. Some pupils will make no progress or may even regress because of associated medical conditions. For this group, experiences are as important as attainment.

How can the MFL teacher help?

- Liaise with parents and TAs.

- Consider the classroom layout.

- Identify possible sensory experiences in your lessons.

- Use additional sensory supports: objects, pictures, fragrances, music, movements, food, etc.

- Take photographs to record experiences and responses.

- Set up a work/subject buddy rota for the class.

- Identify times when the pupil can work with groups.

- Record target language responses on a communication aid.

- Add voice clips in the target language to switch activities on the computer. 'C'est Jacques. Il rit. Il saute.'

MENCAP, 117–123 Golden Lane, London EC1Y 0RT
Tel: 020 7454 0454 Website: http://www.mencap.org.uk

SPECIFIC LEARNING DIFFICULTIES (SpLD)

The term 'specific learning difficulties' covers dyslexia, dyscalculia and dyspraxia.

Dyslexia

The term 'dyslexia' is used to describe a learning difficulty associated with words and it can affect a pupil's ability to read, write and/or spell. Research has shown that there is no one definitive definition of dyslexia or one identified cause, and it has a wide range of symptoms. Although found across a whole range of ability levels, the idea that dyslexia presents as a difficulty between expected outcomes and performance is widely held.

Main characteristics:

- Pupils may frequently lose their place while reading, make a lot of errors with the high frequency words, have difficulty reading names and have difficulty blending sounds and segmenting words. Reading requires a great deal of effort and concentration.

- Pupils' work may seem messy with crossing outs, similarly shaped letters may be confused, such as b/d/p/q, m/w, n/u, and letters in words may be jumbled: tired/tried. Spelling difficulties often persist into adult life and these pupils become reluctant writers.

How can the MFL teacher help?

- Use computers to record work.

- Provide extra practice for spelling new vocabulary.

- Be aware that left/right cause problems in English so double check when working on directions.

- Use computers which have a spellchecker in the target language such as *TextEase*.

- Provide photocopied lists of spellings.

- Look at other ways of recording information, e.g. tapes, mind maps, pictures.

The British Dyslexia Association
Tel: 0118 966 8271 Website: www.bda-dyslexia.org.uk
Dyslexia Institute
Tel: 01784 222 300 Website: www.dyslexia-inst.org.uk

Dyscalculia

Main characteristics:

- The pupil may have difficulty counting by rote, writing or reading numbers, miss out or reverse numbers, have difficulty with mental maths, and be unable to remember concepts, rules and formulae.

- Many have difficulty with money, telling the time, with directions, and with right and left, which are all key MFL topics.

How can the MFL teacher help?

- Encourage the use of rough paper for working out.

- Provide practical objects that are age appropriate to aid learning.

- Allow extra time for tasks, including assessments and examinations.

- There is a lot of number work in learning a language: prices, train times, etc. Provide extra practice in these tasks.

- Provide word lists and photocopies of copying from the board.

- Create activities which involve looking, touching and counting aloud.

- Provide reinforcement for work on left/right, map work and directions.

Website: www.dyscalculia .co.uk

Dyspraxia

The term 'dyspraxia' is used to describe an immaturity with the way in which the brain processes information, resulting in messages not being properly transmitted.

Main characteristics:

- difficulty in co-ordinating movements, may appear awkward and clumsy
- difficulty with handwriting and drawing, throwing and catching
- difficulty following sequential events, e.g. multiple instructions
- may misinterpret situations, take things literally
- limited social skills which result in frustration and irritation
- some articulation difficulties

How can the MFL teacher help?

- Be sensitive to the pupil's limitations in outdoor activities and plan tasks to enable success.
- Ask the pupil questions to check his understanding of instructions/tasks.
- Check seating position to encourage good presentation (both feet resting on the floor, desk at elbow height and, ideally, with a sloping surface to work on).
- Use computers to record work, to minimise handwriting problems.
- Provide buddies for oral work who will be sensitive to needs.

Website: www.dyspraxiafoundation.org.uk

Speech, language and communication difficulties (SLCD)

Pupils with SLCD have problems understanding what others say and/or making others understand what they say. Speech and language difficulties are common in young children but most problems are resolved during the primary years. Problems that persist beyond the transfer to secondary school will be more severe. Any problem affecting speech, language and communication will have a significant effect on a pupil's self-esteem, and personal and social relationships. The development of literacy skills is also likely to be affected. Sign language gives pupils an additional method of communication. Pupils with speech, language and communication difficulties cover the whole range of academic abilities.

Main characteristics:

- **Speech difficulties**
  Pupils who have difficulties with expressive language may experience problems in articulation and the production of speech sounds, or in co-ordinating the muscles that control speech. They may have a stammer or some other form of dysfluency.

- **Language/communication difficulties**
  Pupils with receptive language impairments have difficulty understanding the meaning of what others say. They may use words incorrectly with inappropriate grammatical patterns, have a reduced vocabulary, or find it hard to recall words and express ideas. Some pupils will also have difficulty using and understanding eye contact, facial expression, gesture and body language.

How can the MFL teacher help?

- Talk to parents, speech therapist – and the pupil.
- Learn the most common signs for your subject.
- Use visual supports: objects, pictures, symbols.
- Use the pupil's name when addressing them.
- Give one instruction at a time, using short, simple sentences.
- Give time to respond before repeating a question.
- Make sure pupils understand what they have to do before starting a task.
- Give access to a computer or other IT equipment appropriate to the subject.
- Give written homework instructions.

ICAN, 4 Dyer's Buildings, Holborn, London EC1N 2QP
Tel: 0845 225 4071
Email: info@ican.org.uk Website: http://www.ican.org.uk
AFASIC, 2nd Floor, 50–52 Great Sutton Street, London EC1V 0DJ
Tel: 0845 355 5577 (Helpline) Tel: 020 7490 9410 Fax: 020 7251 2834
Email: info@afasic.org.uk Website: http://www.afasic.org.uk

Tourette's Syndrome (TS)

Tourette's Syndrome is a neurological disorder characterised by tics. Tics are involuntary rapid or sudden movements or sounds that are frequently repeated. There is a wide range of severity of the condition, with some people having no need to seek medical help while others have a socially disabling condition. The tics can be suppressed for a short time but will be more noticeable when the pupil is anxious or excited.

Main characteristics:

- **Physical tics**
  These range from simple blinking or nodding through more complex movements to more extreme conditions such as echopraxia (imitating actions seen) or copropraxia (repeatedly making obscene gestures).

- **Vocal tics**
  Vocal tics may be as simple as throat clearing or coughing but can progress to be as extreme as echolalia (the repetition of what was last heard) or coprolalia (the repetition of obscene words).

Tourette's Syndrome itself causes no behavioural or educational problems but other, associated disorders such as Attention Deficit Hyperactivity Disorder (ADHD) or Obsessive Compulsive Disorder (OCD) may be present.

How can the MFL teacher help?

- Establish a rapport with the pupil.

- Talk to the parents.

- Agree an 'escape route' signal should the tics become disruptive.

- Allow the pupil to sit at the back of the room to prevent staring.

- Give access to a computer to reduce the need for handwriting.

- Make sure the pupil is not teased or bullied.

- Be alert for signs of anxiety or depression.

Tourette Syndrome (UK) Association
PO Box 26149, Dunfermline, KY12 7YU
Tel: 0845 458 1252 (Helpline)
Tel: 01383 629600 (Admin) Fax: 01383 629609
Email: enquiries@tsa.org.uk Website: http://www.tsa.org.uk

CHAPTER 4

The Inclusive MFL Classroom

Brian Howes is a teacher at The Priory School, a secondary school for pupils with moderate learning difficulties and Autistic Spectrum Disorders, which serves a very large area of rural south Lincolnshire. Many teachers will identify with his experience of working with pupils with special needs:

French is hard but he speaks it really well

This fenland countryside is very sparsely populated and the effects of rural deprivation are all too apparent. Many of our pupils have very limited experience or understanding of the world outside their immediate home area. We decided to go camping in France and offered the visit to all our Year 9 pupils, most of whom leapt at the chance. The visits that year and the two years following were a great success, both in terms of the educational experience for the pupils and educating ourselves. However, at the end of one of those weeks, one of our pupils, Lucy, said to her teacher on the ferry home, 'Miss, those French people are really clever, aren't they?' When asked why she thought this, Lucy replied, 'Well, Miss, we've learned a bit of French and it was really hard but those French people all speak it really well!'

Lucy's comment really brought into focus one of the key issues involved in teaching a foreign language to pupils with learning difficulties – even at the age of 14, she had still not fully grasped the idea that people in other countries grow up learning a mother tongue that is different from English.[1]

There are many children in many parts of the country – and not necessarily children with learning difficulties – who have little sense of the world outside their own particular community. Part of the role of all teachers, not just teachers of modern foreign languages, is to give pupils that sense of the wider world and their own place in it.

Why teach MFL to pupils with special needs?

MFL teachers will be familiar with the arguments for and against teaching additional languages to pupils with special needs. One of the avowed intentions of the DfES (2002) publication *Languages for All: Languages for Life, A Strategy for England* was that 'secondary pupils should have high quality teaching and learning at Key Stage 3 and a flexible curriculum and range of routes to support success during the 14–19 phase'.[2]

Some pupils with special needs excel at modern foreign languages as this account of lessons with pupils on the autistic spectrum shows:

French is a popular subject in the communication disorder unit at Hillpark Secondary in Glasgow . . . the pupils have many strengths in favour of language learning. Good rote memory, for example, is ideal for vocabulary learning. Youngsters are keen on routine and this, coupled with a lower level of self-consciousness about speaking out, works well with greetings and instructions in French classes. This lack of self-consciousness brings an added ability to repeat accurately and mimic speech, so a good French accent can develop naturally.[3]

In similar vein, David Wilson, Head of Equal Opportunities and Modern Foreign Languages at Harton School suggests that MFL can enhance rather than detract from literacy:

Our SEN pupils are very indignant if we attempt to withdraw them from MFL lessons. They want to remain with their friends, enjoying what they see as a fun and practical activity. German has a relatively simple spelling system and over the years I've known many young people getting better GCSE results in German than in English . . . Starting from scratch in another language might well be the making of them and lead to an improvement in their mother tongue performance.[4]

Many pupils enjoy learning a language, especially in the early stages and find it exciting and rewarding. It has status in Year 7 and is seen as being something of a rite of passage, part of going up to secondary school.

Each pupil has a right of entitlement to the curriculum, to life experiences, including speaking French, German, Spanish, etc., and to be able to visit these countries. It is an equal opportunity issue.[5]

Basic good practice

Children with special educational needs can find language learning very challenging and so we must make every effort to ensure that they are given as much support as possible. In order to accommodate the varying needs of pupils, a range of strategies will be needed, but basic good practice goes a long way to making the curriculum accessible to all pupils.

There are many practical things which a teacher can do to make life easier for the learner. Remember to make everything explicit:

- Establish routines for opening and ending the lesson: 'Bonjour' . . . 'Au revoir . . .'

- Tell them what you expect: that they will speak in the target language, repeat phrases aloud, listen to one another and do homework.

- Model, explain, practise and reinforce routines.

- Tell them what they have to bring to each class: do not assume they will bring pen, pencils, coloured pencils, paper, etc. Teach them the words for these and check regularly.

- Be clear about when students have choices and what the choices are, e.g. 'Il y a cinq questions. Répondez aux trois.'

- Be clear which things are not optional, e.g. 'Écoutez dans le silence.'

- Plan for appropriate social interaction. How will pair work and group work be incorporated? Careful partnering can make a big difference to pupils with SEN, for example a pupil with a sight impairment may have a well-developed auditory memory. He can be teamed up with pupils who are good writers but lack confidence in oral work. In this way, both parties benefit.

- Be clear about when speaking is good and when it is a distraction.

- Establish norms for noise level in the room, and educate the pupils about this level so that they can take responsibility. Do not shout as this just adds to the noise and confusion. Flick the light switch on and off as a signal that you want the class to be quiet. Not only will this save your voice but also it will attract the attention of pupils with a hearing impairment and those who find it hard to listen.

The atmosphere

Put the group at ease. Emotional support is particularly important in the MFL classroom where pupils may be nervous about learning in a totally new context. Everyone learns best when they are relaxed and feel safe, but language learning, to a certain extent, depends on taking risks. Pupils are encouraged to reach out for unfamiliar words and sounds, and children, especially adolescents, are reluctant to do this if they feel they will be laughed at. The emotional environment within the classroom, then, is particularly important, and teachers need to ensure that pupils are expected to be supportive of one another. Praise pupils who help one another and show good active listening skills.

Use time effectively: structure the lesson so that learning comes in manageable chunks. Provide a structure so that pupils process language and do not just parrot it.

A useful model is:

- PRESENT the language to be learned.

  Explain it and show it. Use colour on the board to bring out key points. Make sure pupils have a handout or have time to copy it down. They need to see, hear and understand. Give slow writers and pupils with sensory impairments a copy of the text so they are working on comprehension, perhaps with a Learning Support Assistant, instead of wasting time copying text very slowly and inaccurately.

- PRACTISE the new structure or vocabulary.

  This means using repetition and Question and Answer to get pupils to repeat the language in the same context in which it was presented. This can work well in the context of a story rather than in unstructured, unrelated examples. For example, if you are teaching the future using aller + infinitive, you might link to daily routines: 'Demain André va se lever à sept heures. Il va manger . . .'

- EXTEND the language practice to new contexts.

  This might draw on previous knowledge or vocabulary from other topics. Once you are confident that pupils understand the structure of aller + infinitive, extend it to: 'Demain André et sa soeur Hélène vont rendre visite à . . .'

- PREPARE for communication.

  Pupils undertake tasks to help them reinforce knowledge. Move away from the story to more varied examples and wider contexts such as holidays, when I leave school, etc.

- PUPILS COMMUNICATE.

  Here pupils make independent use of the new language. Set a task – written or oral but make it clear that you are assessing their ability to use the form aller + infinitive.

Never split the explanation from the practice. Always put grammar and new vocabulary near the beginning of a lesson. If you teach something one lesson and wait till next time to put it into practice, the pupils will have forgotten.

Encourage pupils to develop their curiosity and problem-solving skills. Build a success culture: keep promoting your subject. Be positive, communicate high expectations – that everyone can and should make progress in their language learning. Celebrate their achievements but be honest – don't praise without justification, as pupils will see through that and feel patronised. Some pupils have learned to be helpless, because they have spent much of their life being dependent on adults. They expect parents, siblings, teachers, LSAs and other pupils to make decisions, direct activities and sort out problems. Offer praise for everything that they achieve independently. It may not be a long piece of work or of high quality, but it may be their first solo endeavour and that is worth celebrating.

Managing behaviour

Problems in a mixed-ability class may not be about physical disability or learning difficulty. Often they are more nebulous – the child who won't try, the child with attitude. Pupils with behavioural difficulties come in all shapes and sizes and no single strategy will work for all. The table below shows some characteristics which you may recognise from pupils in your class.

TABLE 4.1 SOME PUPIL BEHAVIOURS

PUPIL BEHAVIOURS	THINK ABOUT
Anti-authority, disruptive, aggressive, swearing, bullying, often out of control	The teacher who is an authority figure is like a red rag to a bull. Shouting, issuing orders, always teaching from the front of the class, using sarcasm, will bring out the worst in these pupils. Go for calm reason. Do not negotiate or change your mind about sanctions.
Unco-operative, clever, calculating, hurt others with their cruel comments	Pupils need to be kept busy to see the relevance of what they are doing to the real world. They want 'street cred' and a sense of achievement on their terms. Sometimes if they do the work, they could well be on the gifted register in some of their subjects.
Attention-seeking, manipulative	These pupils need more action and less listening, more experimentation and problem solving. If they feel rewarded and respected, they can calm down and behave in a more acceptable way which enhances their self-respect.
Unable to sit still, poor attention span, don't finish tasks, difficulty getting organised, easily distracted	Variety of tasks needed. Rewards for keeping on task. Allow them to walk around if vital but try to stop them disrupting others. Use multimedia to capture attention.
Socially isolated, procrastinating, excessively sluggish, difficulty getting started, keep to themselves socially, sensitive to criticism, moody	Pair work could be a good strategy but make these students responsible for getting work done and reporting back.
Depressed, withdrawn, anti-social to rest of class, nervous of new experiences, shy	Pupils in this group often like the immediate feedback that drills and skills activities can provide.

Of course, it is quite different thinking about individual pupils and their needs from dealing with a child who is just one in a class of 30 who all want something different from the teacher. But this case study about Sarah shows what can be done.

Sarah: Year 7

Sarah has a diagnosis of Asperger's Syndrome but her academic achievement so far has been below the average for her age. Sarah had behavioural difficulties at primary school but these have not surfaced since the transfer to secondary. Rather, she has been quiet, withdrawn and anxious, drifting away from the few friends she had in her previous school. Sarah appears to be articulate, but her comprehension of both spoken and written English is poor.

She is working on the 'En Famille' unit (Unit 2 from QCA Schemes of Work). The French teacher needs to make the curriculum relevant and interesting, to differentiate the work so that Sarah can achieve success, and to encourage her to take part in the class as she gains more confidence. Sarah has five hours' support time on her statement of special educational needs. The school uses these hours flexibly to give her support when it is most needed. She had individual support in French for the first term as it was expected that she would find the subject difficult. However, Sarah had no major problems and she obviously enjoyed the subject. As none of the class had studied French before, Sarah quickly realised that she knew as much as anyone else and managed to keep up in class. All the staff had an INSET on Autistic Spectrum Disorders before Sarah transferred. The teacher makes sure that Sarah has written down the homework task and understands what she has to do before she leaves the lesson.

Lesson 1 of the unit: Members of the family and negatives

Class objectives

To ask and answer questions about the names and number of family members, including answers using negatives.

IEP target addressed in this lesson

Sarah will put up her hand and wait when she wants to answer a question.

The lesson

Sarah chose to sit at the front of the class at a single desk by the window. She was reluctant to join in the class activity that started the lesson –

flashcards of an imaginary family – but the teacher asked her several direct questions and she was able to answer, albeit in a very quiet voice.

The pupils then drew and labelled their own family tree. The teacher had put a note in Sarah's homework diary after the previous lesson, asking her to bring in photographs of her family, as she finds drawing very difficult. Sarah stuck these photographs into her book and wrote captions below, some words being copied from the whiteboard.

The teacher paired Sarah with another girl for the next activity, each girl asking and answering questions about the other's family. The teacher had provided prompt cards for the pairs to use. Sarah used these and also pointed to the photographs in her book. The lesson finished with another flashcard game around the class, again about the imaginary family. Sarah was more confident this time and put up her hand twice, answering the question correctly each time.

The physical environment

Factors which militate against an inclusive classroom include poor materials, misunderstandings, lack of communication and inappropriate teaching methods. The layout of the classroom is another key aspect. Look at the layout of the room and consider how you could improve it. Is it easy for the class to work in pairs without having to move lots of furniture? Is there an area that can be used for role play? Is there a quiet area? Look at equipment. If you are using language masters, are they easy to get out? Is anyone using a laptop for access? Megan is in a wheelchair and uses a laptop to help record her work. She needs to be within easy reach of a power point as her battery may well go down.

Often the room is full of equipment – realia, maps and pictures and, while this can provide a visually stimulating environment, it can also provide sensory overload, particularly for any pupils with Autistic Spectrum Disorders. These youngsters can find it difficult to concentrate in the face of even minor distractions. Make one corner a stimulus-free area where people can sit and think or engage in quiet study. Make sure that this is not seen as 'the naughty corner', but a place where pupils routinely go to work alone or in pairs.

Sit at a table in your classroom and look at the language environment from a pupil perspective:

- Have you covered every square inch of wall space with pupil work as a way of celebrating achievement?

- Do wall displays link to particular parts of the curriculum?

- Have you remembered that font size and clarity are important if texts are to be read from various points in the classroom by pupils with a visual impairment and by pupils who are struggling with the demands of the language?

Bhavini has limited sight. The class were looking at a display with photos and magazine articles about a spectacular concert in Barcelona, featuring some of their favourite artists. She stayed sitting at her desk as she knew she would not be able to see it. At break, the teacher asked Steven if he would like to earn a merit by staying behind and showing the display to Bhavini. As he has behavioural problems he was quite surprised that he had been chosen. He explained each picture to Bhavini and read out some of the text. Once or twice when he struggled to read a word, she helped him, as she has a better vocabulary and knowledge of the language. Together they made sense of the display and enjoyed helping each other.

Change displays often. They lose their appeal quite quickly. Encourage pupils to make things for the wall. They often remember things they have touched and constructed much more clearly than pieces of writing. Perhaps take a theme for a wall and use it as a stimulus for all years, for example create a character on the wall. Pupils may use this for simple things such as name, age: 'Pierre a dix ans', etc., as a focus for adjectives and descriptions, or for negatives: 'Mme Dupont n'est plus jeune'. Pupils can create narratives which might focus on themes such as holidays or going to the doctor, or on more outlandish topics such as witnessing a bank robbery, which could reinforce questions, imperatives and numbers. Younger pupils will see the language work of older classes and may be able to guess at some of the words, while older pupils will be revisiting some structures and simple vocabulary when they see what pupils in Year 7 have created.

Interactive whiteboards

Interactive whiteboards are becoming increasingly popular. They are great tools for language work because:

- It is easier to integrate sound and video as part of the lesson. This can more clearly demonstrate the relationship between the written word and what is heard.

- Colour and pictures reach out to a wider range of learning styles, so those who are visual learners can benefit greatly.

- The printout facility can help to reinforce messages and encourage peer discussion. Printouts are especially useful for pupils with dyslexia, who copy inaccurately and may have short-term memory problems.

However, they are not a universal remedy for all pupils. There are a number of issues which affect pupils with special needs, not least Health and Safety:

- Classrooms are not designed for interactive whiteboards so they may not be well sited.

- Can all pupils see clearly or do you need to make sure that a child with a visual impairment is not being dazzled?

- Research suggests that the whiteboard leads to a faster pace of lesson and this may not suit those who need time for ideas and vocabulary to sink in.

For a fuller account of the research, see Appendix 4.1.

Making print materials more accessible

Most of the materials you use in the MFL classroom are likely to be paper-based. MFL books are generally lively and fun with lots of busy pictures, cartoons and illustrations. They work well for the majority of pupils because the text is broken up into bite size chunks so they do not get bored or lose their place. However, this style of presentation can be a problem for some learners with dyslexia and those who have particular eye conditions. If you talk about 'the picture in the bottom right corner', hold the book up and show the class where it is. Often pupils with dyslexia have particular problems with left and right and may spend ages puzzling over the wrong picture.

Illustrations are a vital ingredient, whether they are photographs, drawings or cartoons. They motivate most pupils, and in many cases give visual clues to the accompanying text. This is helpful to all learners, especially those who have a strong visual memory; illustrations also 'break up' text into more manageable chunks.

Many pupils find reading difficult for a whole variety of reasons. The majority of texts are still black print on a white background, and this is uncomfortable for some categories of readers. Pupils with dyslexia may use a coloured plastic overlay to obviate the problem of 'glare'. However, they still may find it harder to write on white paper. Schools could ease this problem by making paper available in a range of colours for homework or 'best work'.

Producing your own materials

Here are some guidelines for creating handouts:

TABLE 4.2 CREATING HANDOUTS

Fonts	Arial, Comic Sans, Sassoon and New Century Schoolbook are easier to read than other fonts.
Font size	12 or 14 is best for most pupils.
Font format	**Bold** is OK; *italic* is hard to read.
Spacing	Use double or 1.5 line spacing to help pupils who have problems with visual tracking.
Layout of materials	Use lots of headings and subheadings as signposts.
CAPITAL LETTERS	These are hard to read so use sparingly.
Consistency	Ensure instructions and symbols are used consistently.
Provide answers	If pupils can check answers for themselves, they learn more and become more independent.
Enlarging	It is better to enlarge text by using a bigger font on a word processor rather than relying on the photocopier. Photocopied enlargements can appear fuzzy and A3 paper never fits neatly in exercise books or folders.
Forms	If you are making an identity card or something similar, remember that partially sighted pupils often have handwriting that is larger than average, so allow extra space on forms. This will also help pupils with learning difficulties who have immature or poorly formed writing or are still printing.
Spacing	Keep to the same amount of space between each word. Do not use justified text as the uneven word spacing can make reading more difficult.
Alignment	Align text to the left margin. This makes it easier to find the start and finish of each line. It ensures an even space between each word.
Columns	Make sure the margin between columns clearly separates them.
Placing illustrations	Do not wrap text around images if it means that lines of text will start in different places. Do not have text going over images as this makes it hard to read.

See Appendix 4.2 for examples of good and bad worksheets.

Making materials for pupils who are blind or visually impaired can cause some headaches for teachers but as the following extract about flashcards from *Willkommen in der Klasse!* shows, there are ways round the problem:

Flashcards

If you are using flashcards, children with visual impairment will need alternative ways to access the information you are holding up. Firstly, don't waste your time (or the VI support team's time) producing tactile versions of picture flashcards – the focus group assure me that it takes up a disproportionately large amount of time for little or no return, and the flashcards can be very confusing!

Consider the alternatives listed here instead:

- Partially sighted children may be able to see the cards if they are at the front of the class. Consider having an identical set of cards for a support assistant to duplicate what you are holding up.
- Ask a child's sighted friend or their support assistant to whisper (in English) what is on the card.

Use of tape

Tape work may be accessible to all children in your class, but if so, bear in mind the following points:

- If a child is recording answers with a Perkins brailler, you will need to stop the tape so that the child has the opportunity to write their answer without clattering keys over the next bit of tape dialogue (sighted children would write their answer silently as they hear it).

- Alternatively, the visually impaired child could whisper their answer to their support assistant who would then write it down. This works particularly well for tick box questions. But again, you will have to make judicial use of the pause button to allow the child to whisper their answer without missing out on crucial dialogue.

- A sighted child and a visually impaired child could work as a pair, using the same method as above, but taking it in turns to answer the question.

Some other ideas

Many visually impaired children have well-developed memory skills and team games can capitalise on this, using the sight of a sighted child, and the oral and listening skills of a blind or partially sighted child to report back.[6]

Supporting writing

Most pupils find writing hard. It requires concentration, the ability to work for quite a long period, to remember sets of instructions, to come up with ideas, to recall the language, to write it down. It may possibly require the pupil to check, edit and alter it, and finally to remember to hand it in. Unlike speaking and listening, it may cover a long timescale. The gap between being told to write the text for a letter or email to handing it in may be well over a week. For pupils who have literacy problems in their first language, writing in a foreign language can seem daunting.

Think about motivating pupils. Keep written activities short. It is better for them to write six phrases on different topics which 'grab' them than to struggle through half a page on a subject that has no appeal. Work up to writing slowly.

The priorities with beginner writers are:

- To build up confidence and to change the learner's attitude from 'I can't do this' to 'I'll have a go at it.'

- To build up a basic range of words they can use with confidence.

Cloze is a useful activity. The teacher chooses a passage, removes some of the words and draws a line in the gap. The reader has to fill in the missing words. You can make the activity easier by listing all the missing words at the bottom of the page (see page 55).

The student can be asked to summarise the story/dialogue using as few words as possible. One way of starting this activity is to get the student to tell someone else the story. Ask them to check through the text and then write a few questions. These questions could be used by other students in the future but, more importantly, the effort of writing the questions increases understanding and confidence in handling the text. Give them some vocabulary to get them started. You could make it a whole-class activity to generate a suitable list.

Students should be taught the language of opinion so that they can say what they think about a topic under discussion. They should also be shown real writing, such as simple advertisements in the target language, captions and emails. They need to know languages are for life, not just for school!

french1 - ClozePro

File Edit View Insert Format Options Help

Après le déjeuner, tout le _____ commence au travail. Jean passe

l'aspirateur, Emma fait la vaisselle et Mme Laigle fait un peu de _____

Vingt minutes _____, Jean dit, "J'ai passé l'aspirateur dans ma _____

et la salle à manger. Est-ce que je _____ sortir?"

"Mais non, mon _____," dit sa mère, "tu ne peux pas _____. Tu n'as

pas _____ ta chambre et puis tu _____ aller à la boucherie. J'ai _____

d'un gigot _____."

chambre	petit	lessive
besoin	peux	rangé	d'agneau
après	monde	sortir

Mots

Start | french1 - Cl... | Microsoft Wo... 16:35

Multi-sensory language learning

We may have a hundred and one reasons to explain why pupils do not learn: 'He doesn't work hard enough', 'She has a disruptive home life', 'He is disorganised', 'She is deaf', 'He is dyslexic', 'She's never in school'. What we don't know most of the time is how people do learn. No one is born knowing a language. Certainly some pupils have an aptitude for language learning: some find reading easy, some are good at acquiring new vocabulary, or seem to assimilate syntax effortlessly, or have a good accent, or find ways of linking new knowledge to previously learnt material. But what makes knowledge stick? Certainly the more channels we use in teaching, the more likely we are to help pupils learn. Many pupils are very artistic, creative and imaginative, so these characteristics can be exploited in language learning:

- Pupils may have a strong eye for colour – vocabulary could be blue for masculine, red/pink for feminine. Some teachers use different colours for different tenses.

- Grammar may be an alien concept. Do not assume pupils understand singular/plural. Try to reinforce this pictorially. Not all children will understand the concept of a past tense. BSL and some community languages do not have a separate form for things which happened in the past. Give an explanation and an example, and put it into practice at once. Learning needs to be in small chunks, with lots of repetition at regular intervals. Remember: 'Children are not slow learners but they are quick forgetters.'

- When learning set phrases, chanting may be helpful as the rhythm can act as a reinforcement. Encourage pupils to make up songs (with actions) to familiar tunes such as 'Here we go gathering nuts in May'. This can help embed lots of new vocabulary, as in the hypochondriac's song:

  'Bonjour Monsieur, J'ai mal à la tête, mal à la tête, mal à la tête . . .
  Oh Monsieur, J'ai mal à la tête! Oh la la la la!
  Bonjour Monsieur, J'ai mal à la gorge! . . .'

- Set the scene – get pupils to envisage what sort of language is likely to come up. If two people are meeting for the first time, we can expect greetings, names, etc. If a passage has the word 'gare', we can look out for numbers, times and destinations.

- Talk about the country and the culture to make it all more interesting, e.g. tell them that in France, children leave their shoes out in the hope of getting presents for la Fête des Rois.

- Humour helps. Most children cannot understand the funny cartoons thoughtfully provided by authors of MFL textbooks, but print out a Simpson strip from the Web and they will try very hard to work out the meaning. It's funny, it's relevant, and they have a context for the language.

● Use sound. Teachers can pre-record a tape with explanations of key grammar points. A pupil can listen to it again and again. Or make a PowerPoint demonstration. There are lots on the Teacher's Resource Exchange[7] which you can download. Then they can look, listen and maybe interact with the slides. It is sometimes claimed that a student with dyslexia needs to 'overlearn' material up to 30 times before it becomes properly implanted.

● There are some talking word processors such as *Textease*[8] which can speak French and German. Linking word and sound helps with some pupils' learning. *Textease* also has a library of simple clipart type pictures which can reinforce vocabulary.

● Use art. Pupils can learn by doing. Use an art package to create adverts or posters. One useful activity is to teach body vocabulary through drawing. Get pupils to draw a monster and describe it: 'Tiene tres ojos amarillos', 'un nariz azul', etc.

● If possible have a foreign cookery day, working with recipes in the target language.

Remember that your main objective is to make pupils confident in their ability to understand and communicate. So I will end this chapter with an anecdote. I was once on a coach trip to Spain where we stopped for a break at a service station some miles south of Paris. Many of the adults held back and muttered among themselves, not daring to try and buy anything as it would involve speaking French and they might lose face. A boy with Down's Syndrome stepped forward and asked for 'deux croissants et un café s'il vous plait'. He then emptied out his pockets, scattering notes and small change in several currencies. The cashier helped him pick it up, extracted the right money and he was on his way with his food. The adults went hungry whilst he enjoyed his breakfast. What excellent communication and life skills! His teacher could be very proud.

Notes

1 Howes, B. (June 2001) 'Those French people are really clever', *Special Children*, Questions Publishing.

2 DfES (2002) *Languages for All: Languages for Life, A Strategy for England.* This document can be downloaded at www.dfes.gov.uk/languagesstrategy

3 Caldwell, E. 'A difficulty, oui, but a deficit, non', *TES Scotland*, 10 May 2002.

4 Wilson, D. (July 2003) 'Accessing the secondary school curriculum': Senco-forumlists.becta.org.uk/pipermail/senco-forum/2003-July/032283.html

5 Bovair, K. (Autumn 2002) 'I suppose', The CILT bulletin *MFL*, 1, 7.

6 'Willkommen in der Klasse!' Reproduced with kind permission from Curriculum Close Up, the newsletter of the RNIB Curriculum Information Service (01905 357635).

7 Teacher Resource Exchange: tre-ngfl.gov.uk

8 Textease: Softease Ltd., Market Place, Ashbourne, Derbyshire, DE6 1ES.

CHAPTER 5

Teaching and Learning Styles

I am an NQT in MFL who trained in a school with set classes. My new school has mixed ability groups. How can I ensure that every pupil's learning needs are catered for, in particular those with SEN? Differentiating tasks tends to mean that planning my lessons can take a very long time. Is there any advice on how to effectively plan and teach lessons to the benefit of all pupils in a mixed-ability teaching group?[1]

An inclusive classroom is very hard to define but it is about developing the least restrictive environment. Not every child is going to be able to do all the four competencies of speaking, listening, reading and writing equally well. It is very much about differentiation and enabling pupils to show what they can do instead of what they can't. But it needs a change in mindset by teachers:

Time is the reason why so many teachers feel that they cannot differentiate whether it is by task or outcome . . . This is because teachers see differentiation as extra and not part of the delivery of the curriculum[2] (McNamara and Moreton 1997).

One of the first things that teachers need to realise is that a mixed-ability group means exactly what it says: the group has a mixture of abilities. This is quite different from seeing the class as a group of average and able children, with a subset of children who have problems. Pupils have all sorts of strengths which can be exploited to benefit one another. A pupil with a visual impairment may have poor spelling and be slow to produce written work but may have a fantastic aural memory and a wonderful capacity to absorb and speak the language. A child with limited hearing may find it hard to reproduce the sounds needed for French, German or Spanish, but may have developed a host of study skills for decoding meaning from unfamiliar words and find it easy to transfer these skills to other languages. All pupils can learn from each other. The classroom model should be:

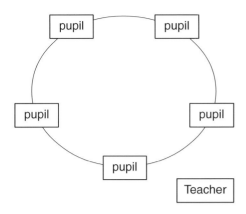

The teacher is not the central focus but rather a guide, time keeper and resource provider to help learning take place effectively. This role may mark a change for some teachers who fear they will lose control if they adopt more learner-centred styles of teaching.

Learning styles

People learn in different ways and, in the past, schools focused very much on a reading and writing approach to grammar and vocabulary. Through research on literacy and thinking skills, we have come to realise that there are many different routes to the same goal. Yet often this does transfer to classroom practice. Some pupils simply do not learn if they are sitting down! Somehow movement stimulates the brain. Yet pupils are constantly told to stop wandering about the room and get back to their seats.

In 1981 Roger Sperry won the Nobel Peace Prize for his experimentation on left-brain and right-brain hemisphere brain functions. He discovered that most of us use both sides of our brain, but have a bias to one side or the other. Traditional academia is very left brained with an emphasis on words, details, and categorising. The right side of the brain focuses on non-verbal and intuitive ways of working.

TABLE 5.1 LEFT AND RIGHT BRAIN LEARNING STYLES

LEFT BRAIN EMPHASISES:	RIGHT BRAIN EMPHASISES:
language	images
rules and grammar	awareness of shape
mathematical formulae	appreciation of patterns
numbers	able to work in three dimensions
sequences	rhythm and musical appreciation
linearity	seeing the whole picture
analysis	

It might seem at first glance as if only traditionally academic, left-brained children are going to make a success of their language learning, but we know that is not true. Otherwise, every school would have hundreds of right-brained children, totally unable to communicate in their first language. Many children, if stimulated with appropriate visual or auditory prompts, make an enormous leap in language acquisition. They are no better or worse than left-brained children; they just have different strengths and weaknesses.

A good teacher needs to be flexible and to take account of differing learning styles. 'Visual' learners will benefit from pictures and flashcards. Put up part of a picture on a whiteboard or OHP and get pupils to call out what they think it is. You will be pleasantly surprised at how much language knowledge they demonstrate. This gives you the chance to improve their pronunciation and endings if necessary while praising them for the effort.

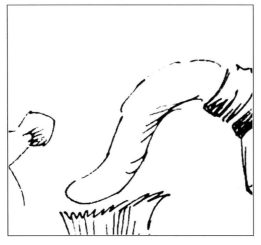

Qu'est-ce que vous voyez? Blanc? Bleu? Lignes?

Oui. Brosse? Très bien – une brosse . . . Alors qu'est-ce que vous voyez?

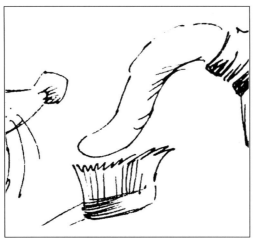

Une brosse aux dents. Oui et . . . oui, c'est le dentifrice. Et

maintenant? Oui, c'est un animal. Un lapin? Peut-être . . .

See Appendix 5.1 for more pictures.

Talking dice is a popular product for improving and developing speaking and listening skills. With each throw of the dice, pupils are encouraged to let their imaginations roll. One set of pupils used them to discuss where they went on holiday; another for talking about things they liked and disliked, giving reasons. Teachers report that it encourages random, spontaneous language which works well for vocabulary, grammar, sentence building, story telling and discussion.[3]

'Auditory' learners will learn from listening and speaking rather than looking and reading. It might be possible to give them tapes to take home to learn vocabulary or structures. Make sure that 'kinaesthetic' learners, who learn by touching and doing, get enough physical activity, perhaps by manipulating chunks of language on cards or by miming activities to fix a connection between their action and the language being learned. This is a lot of work, but you will find that once you have a range of resources for different KS3 and KS4 topics, they can be re-used. Even more importantly, you will develop a different way of thinking so that often it becomes second nature to think of different ways of revisiting the same points. Once you have created the right range of resources, which tap into pupils' different aptitudes, you will enable them to work independently. See Appendix 5.2 for useful resources.

Teaching strategies

Pupils will come into the room with all sorts of other things in their head. Concentration may be better in the morning than in the afternoon when they are getting tired. Alternatively, some classes are very sluggish during the first period. Some pupils may find it difficult to settle down on Monday mornings after the weekend. Sometimes they are 'on a high' after a particular lesson such as drama.

There needs to be some sort of active learning in each lesson, whether it is writing or a tactile activity or a role play or multimedia work. Pupils need to see it, hear it, say it, touch it, taste it or smell it. Languages lend themselves to auditory exercises or visual games, to role play, pair work, and group work. Languages can incorporate number work, poetry, advertisements, football scores, map work, songs and whole class chanting. Resources like newspapers and magazines taken from the language's country of origin can be especially useful.

Set routines and expectations. Ensure that students know what they are supposed to 'pull out of their bag'. If you have a short, sharp activity to work on it will help to settle them down and focus attention, as well as providing a reason to get out pens and exercise books.

It might be that each lesson pupils have to note the date and the weather. If you are working on food then for three weeks perhaps they need to write down at the start of each lesson what they had for tea the previous night. On the other hand, the tasks might change.

'List 6' is a useful quick starter. Here the pupils have to make a list of six things. These might be colours, things you would take on a picnic, items in your suitcase, school subjects or parts of the body. Those with limited language skills should be encouraged to produce a minimum of three things. This task should be accomplished quickly. It should set the pace of the lesson, tune pupils into the language, and get them to focus. It is a 'doing', rather than a listening or looking activity. Other activities are listed in Appendix 5.3.

Good practice guide

- Where possible try to incorporate some reading, writing, speaking and listening in each lesson. This could just be a few words or sentences but it is important to cover the different learning styles.

- Offer the students a choice of activities if possible. Some pupils are good at learning from a book or worksheet; others learn by speaking a language.

- Encourage all students to highlight words or phrases they are unsure about and make them active participants in the learning process.

- Talk about how students will find the answer (apart from asking you!). Can they guess the word? Do they know a similar phrase? Can they make sense of the sentence without that word? What does it say in the glossary? Can they find it in the dictionary?

- Remember the aim is to give them strategies to cope when they are faced with a similar situation in real life, and there's no teacher to hand.

Good direct teaching is achieved by balancing different elements:

Directing	Sharing teaching objectives with the class, ensuring that pupils know what to do, and drawing attention to points over which they should take particular care. Make sure the pace of the lesson is brisk but not too fast.
Instructing	Giving information and structuring it well in small chunks. Ensure practice follows instruction to embed language and concepts.
Demonstrating	Showing pupils what to do, modelling the language and giving clear examples.
Explaining and illustrating	Showing what a good response is and why. Where possible try to link to previous work so pupils have hooks to hang new learning on.
Questioning	Using open and closed questions; questioning in ways which match the direction and pace of the lesson and ensure that all pupils take part. Give examples and remember to say the pupil's name before asking the question, to alert him and give him every chance of providing a good answer. Build in 'thinking time', rather than expecting an immediate response.
Discussing	Responding constructively to pupils; ensuring that pupils of all abilities are involved and contribute to discussions, allowing pupils time to think through answers before inviting a response. Think about altering the seating arrangements to facilitate discussion.
Consolidating	Finding opportunities to reinforce and develop what has been taught, through a variety of activities in class and well-focused tasks to do at home.
Plenary	Ask the question: 'What do you know/can you do that you didn't know/couldn't do before today?' and get members of the group to offer suggestions.

Finishing off

Use the final five or ten minutes of your session to consolidate the group learning. Re-cap your main aims with additional examples, and try to find an imaginative way to assess outcomes for individuals. One approach is to get pupils to discuss in pairs what they think they have learnt that day, how it links to previous work and what they need to remember. Alternatively, choose one or two pupils to be the 'expert' and take questions from the rest of the class. Pupils spend a few minutes preparing a question for the rest of the class. Doing this helps them focus on the purpose of the lesson and provides good feedback for the teacher.

Differentiation by resource

There are very few MFL teachers who just rely on a textbook. These days it is easy to get hold of materials from magazines, tapes, videos, travel books, CD-ROMs and websites. The real question is how do you decide what to take into the classroom?

Ideally, you need real objects for pupils to touch and handle and talk about: 'La jupe est verte. Elle est longue.' The whole process then becomes concrete and multi-sensory as pupils see and touch the object, and hear and speak the language. However, it is not always possible to take in real objects for each lesson. Pictures help for all sorts of reasons. They remove the translation process. If a pupil sees an item and thinks of it in a second language then a link is made, but if he is always thinking of English words and translating them into the target language there is a barrier to learning.

Symbols and pictures can make difficult concepts visible and therefore easier for pupils to understand. Pupils need a context. Lots of struggling readers can decode words once they know what they are looking at. If they see a picture of a football match, they can start to make guesses about unfamiliar vocabulary, such as 'le terrain', 'marquer un but', 'l'arbitre'.

But do choose pictures carefully. Relevance and clarity are crucial – they need to enhance text rather than distract. Make sure that pictures are near enough to the relevant passage, but not so near that they encroach on white space. Not all pupils are graphically literate and, while you may think that the picture is self-evident, it may be too busy for the pupil to pick out the message. Think about what you want the picture to do. Is it just to set the scene and provide a context? Is it to tell a story, or to provide an imaginative stimulus for extended writing, or is it to illustrate particular words and phrases? For a pupil such as Susan, who has communication and language difficulties, the picture of a bedroom does not

conjure up the idea of furniture and describing your own or an ideal bedroom. It suggests bedtime stories, and you may find yourself off at a tangent with the three little pigs. By the time you have digressed into 'Les Trois Petits Cochons', you may be off on animal vocabulary, and have lost the thread of your lesson. It is often assumed that pupils respond better to pictures than to words: 'One picture is worth a thousand words'. Just remember that for some pupils that is at least 900 too many!

Make sure you select resources with appropriate reading levels. One simple test is to choose an exercise or passage of about six lines. If there are more than ten words the pupil doesn't know or can't remember, the work is too hard. Often realia such as menus and packing is very attractive, but the text may not be accessible to some pupils. Make sure that labels on diagrams, maps and illustrations do not cross the lines of the drawing. This deprives the word of its recognisable shape. Even changes in colour or texture under a word can make it more difficult to read.

A checklist for evaluating materials

And, finally – a checklist based on work by some Lancashire support teachers will help you look at course content and resources when differentiating materials for pupils with a wide range of learning needs.

Content

- Can the core content be reduced?
- Is it easy to extend it?
- Is there an appropriate alternative to this core?

Layout

- Can work be spread out over more pages?
- Is work in clear print, e.g. word processed in a sans-serif font?
- Are there line breaks in appropriate places?
- Could there be more emphasis on key words?
- Is sufficient white space used?

Vocabulary

- Can you provide a word bank for revision/introduction of core vocabulary?
- Have you got a further vocabulary list for increasing the complexity of discussion and recording?
- Are there any extra opportunities to practise using/reading/spelling the new vocabulary in a motivating context?
- Do you provide opportunities to revisit essential vocabulary?
- Do you offer creative as well as analytical activities for using vocabulary?

Reading

- Could there be a simpler version?

- Are there opportunities for more illustrations?

- Would symbols add meaning? Could these be developed by the class?

- Could content be tape recorded or videoed?

- Can pupils work in pairs so that competent readers can help others?

- Is text in electronic format? Text to speech software could be used.

- Are there extra resources (CD-ROMs, reference books at a variety of levels, extension worksheets) for strugglers and quick finishers?

Matching tasks to student abilities, aptitudes and interests

Students work in a variety of ways and bring different abilities and aptitudes to that work. One form of differentiation is to provide a variety of tasks that cover the main content area in order to cater for the variety of individuals in the class.

Food vocabulary can be covered in different ways: through vocabulary lists, exercises in a book or formal instruction. Alternatively, the same vocabulary can be covered by drawing out the most relevant vocabulary for pupils by getting them talking: devising menus, discussing their own eating habits, etc.

Sample lesson

Teaching food vocabulary and preferences

1. Make a list of about 40 different foods with pictures.

2. Children choose foods they like or dislike.

3. Make a preferences sheet. This will vary according to the abilities of the children. One group will just select foods and put them in two columns: j'aime, je déteste; other groups will have extra structures to use.

GROUP 1	GROUP 2	GROUP 3
J'aime	+ mais je préfère	+ je n'aime pas
Je déteste	+ J'adore	+ mais je ne déteste pas non plus

Letting children choose their own foods does run the risk that they will not cover all food areas. Many may lack fruit and vegetables! But it will be real and, by letting them pick food words for themselves, they invest more time and thought in the process and are more likely to remember.

Building learning routes

Improve pupils' word recognition skills by creating wordworms on the computer by running words together and removing accents and punctuation. Even better, get them to create wordworms for others. Pupils have to recreate the text by working out where words begin and end. This involves close reading and is a good test of comprehension and grammar skills. It's an excellent collaborative exercise:

Jaimelesframboisesmaisjedetestelespommes

Let them learn by looking and listening. Use a *Clicker* grid that combines pictures with sound. Click on the illustration and you can hear the word in English or French.

Pupils can create sentences by pressing a grid with simple words and structures. Three clicks and a pupil can produce and hear a sentence such as, 'Je voudrais du chocolat s'il vous plaît'.

Use drama strategies to enliven learning. Pupils mime actions to a simple narrative told by the teacher. Use simple props to create a character – a waiter, a businessman in a hurry. Create a setting – A half-eaten meal is on a table. What can we deduce about this person from the clues? Is it a man or a woman? Age?

Lifestyle? Pupils respond to the same task but at different levels and perhaps in pairs or groups.

Alter the setting for your teaching – not all learning takes place in a classroom. Key Stage 3 pupils from a school in Coventry worked on a French food project with a special needs teacher. These pupils required high levels of support and had made least progress with the language. They visited a supermarket and took digital photographs of fruit displays etc., and they went to the local market to take photographs of stalls and cafés. They used a multimedia package to combine these pictures with recordings of their voices and that of the French assistante: 'Voici les oranges', 'J'ai deux pommes', and so on.

After three weeks they rejoined the main group to find that their vocabulary was considerably wider and their pronunciation better than the rest of the class. They had also made a resource for the MFL department which was widely admired and this made them feel useful and valued.

This exercise may be difficult to replicate with a large group but certainly time spent in a real-life situation, perhaps with an LSA or a language assistant, is very worthwhile. Many towns have a French market for a few days each year and if it is not possible to take the whole class, you could see if the market holder would come to the school to talk for a small fee.

A range of tasks to allow choice

When designing tasks, it is important to allow for different starting points for pupils' varying abilities. Remember also to provide variety in type, level, media, skills and styles. Engage creative as well as analytical strategies for decoding and recall. Letting pupils choose the tasks that they carry out will enable them to develop their differing aptitudes and interests. Encourage plenty of consultation to minimise pupils' making unsuitable choices. Encourage as much participation as possible in both planning and instruction.

Cut a simple narrative into sections and ask pupils to organise it into a sequence that pleases them. They could then add illustrations and create their own book. Compare versions made by the class and consider which are more successful and why. These adapt well to working on computer screen where the finished documents can then be printed. Simple cut and paste techniques allow for re-arrangement of the text, and the undo facility allows for retracing steps.

Analytical and creative activities

There are various ways of revisiting vocabulary. You could get the pupils to divide food into things they eat at home and things they buy outside.

Chez moi	J'achète
Pommes de terre	Frites
La viande	Le poisson
Le fromage	Pizza

You could ask them to choose eight to ten of their food words and put them on a continuum from breakfast to dinner, thinking about when in the day they are most likely to eat them, e.g:

Pain grillé, du café, les oeufs, les saucissons, du fromage, frites, du riz, du vin, gateau.

Le petit déjeuner -
Le déjeuner -

Other pupils could put words in alphabetical order as reinforcement of dictionary skills. Some pupils will need an alphabet line where letters are written across the top of the page to do this successfully.

Creative activities might include: role play, making menus on the word processor using clip art and borders, a design an exotic pizza competition or running a French food stall for Comic Relief. There are examples of homework activities in Appendix 5.4.

Differentiation by support

We know that some students need more help than others to complete a given task. If we provide help we are also providing differentiation by support. The strategies suggested in this section provide guidance on how differentiation by support may be given more systematically. Pupils work in a variety of ways and bring different abilities and aptitudes to that work. One form of differentiation is to provide a variety of tasks that cover the main content area in order to cater for the needs of individuals in the class. Some pupils need more help than others to complete a task. It is necessary to consider:

- individual support from the teacher

- small group tutoring

- support from other adults and students

- support from technology

At its simplest, differentiation by support may come down to the discussions that you have with your students. Whilst support for individual students is a vital ingredient in differentiated teaching, do bear in mind the constraints:

- You can't teach each pupil separately.

- Some pupils don't like one-to-one conversations with the teacher.

- Pupils taught separately are not being included in the group.

Small group tutoring may be better. Here you work with a small group for part of the lesson. They are still interacting with other pupils and are learning ways of working without constant one-to-one attention. In some cases, the pupil needs support for some parts of the course but is able to work more independently at other times. Change the pace of the lesson to make sure that pupils understand the concept being presented. One of the things we often overlook in the classroom is that some pupils just need extra time to explore, create, question and experience as they learn.

Support from adults and other pupils

Sometimes support is needed for recording. Teachers often provide handouts for some of the pupils but rely on them to jot down homework, and then wonder why it does not get done. Perhaps TAs could be made available to assist at this point. Could a good note-taker be used in paired or group work? Could pupils sometimes use a tape recorder or video for reporting results, recording facts, keeping notes, telling stories, and so on? Could there be electronic versions of worksheets? Is a clickable grid appropriate? Should it have words, phrases or symbols?

The role of the Learning Support Assistant (LSA) will be covered in Chapter 7. At the very least, an LSA can provide a very welcome extra pair of hands and a listening ear. At best, they provide expertise in matching a task to the individual student. However, it is very important that the teacher monitors this and does not abnegate responsibility for that particular student.

Support from technology

Technology can be used to present information, to help interpret it and to increase student independence in recording work. The following are excellent ways of linking picture and word:

- Get pictures from the 'Royalty-Free Clip Art Collection for Foreign/Second Language Instruction' at http://www.sla.purdue.edu/fll/japanproj/flclipart/.

- Use a word-processing package with pictures or symbols, such as *Clicker*.

- Use *Writing with Symbols* or *Inclusive Writer*.

- Clip art can be used to illustrate ideas or vocabulary.

- Images and digital videos are stimulating and appeal to visual learners.

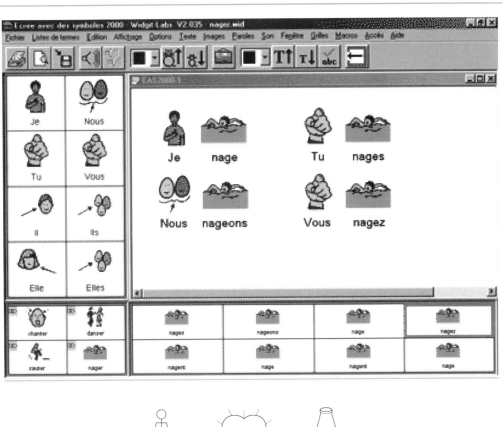

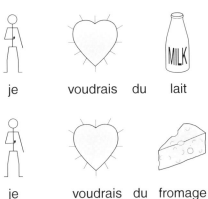

Pupils learn to link the written and spoken word and seem to learn vocabulary and structures much faster this way. The following are suggestions of ways in which you can capitalise on this fact:

- *Textease* has language packs which can be incorporated into their whole suite of word processing and DTP packages which can read text out loud in French or German.

- A talking word processor such as *Textease* can create documents, spell check pupils' work in the target language and read the text back in French or German.

- If text is in an electronic form it can be read by a talking word processor, printed out in Braille, made huge, or split up into manageable chunks.

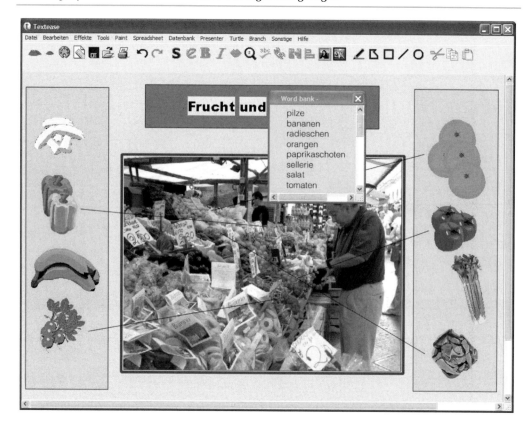

Word-processing packages have many uses:

- Word processing can support those pupils with literacy problems who write very slowly and find it difficult to form letters.

- A word-processing package helps teachers present their work more effectively, making it easy for the teacher to adapt a basic worksheet to simplify or amplify it.

- Use a word processor for cloze exercises, drag and drop or sentence reordering, using colour to highlight past tenses.

- Spreadsheets are a good way to revisit food vocabulary and cost a meal or a party.

- Databases can be used for personal description or hobbies. *Information Workshop* and *Pinpoint* are popular choices for the MFL classroom.

Other recommended software packages include:

- Text manipulation software which can be used to revisit grammatical structures.

- Drill and practice programs which cover grammatical points. Some pupils benefit from focusing on a narrow subset of skills, such as forming past participles, until they are well internalised and they can use them without thinking. Other pupils work through this sort of program very fast but no learning takes place because they are not able to transfer their skills to other contexts.

- Mind-mapping software, such as *Inspiration, Kidspiration* and *DraftBuilder,* can help build up letters and documents on the board as a whole class activity.

- Presentation software such as *PowerPoint* can be a really visual way to introduce new vocabulary or explain grammar points.

Some final suggestions:

- Websites in authentic target language can motivate students by making language learning seem real.

- Web-based interactive games using authoring software such as *Quia, Hot Potatoes, WIDA Authoring Suite* are an enjoyable way of learning.

- CD-ROMs (*Unterwegs, En Route, Métro*) can be useful. The multimedia nature of much of this information makes it accessible to pupils of all abilities. There are also fun materials such as Living Books CD-ROMs (for example, *Grandma and Me*), in some languages.

- Email can be a fun way of linking your class to a school abroad or even to a school in another part of Britain.

Differentiation by response

In the 'old days', teachers usually had one set of responses to pupils – a grade and a written comment. This still has its place – in fact we often are encouraged to give marks and to match pupils' achievement to a set of criteria or statements. But this may not be particularly meaningful to the pupils themselves. We need to consider how we record and evaluate work and find ways of exploiting:

- individual action plans

- pairs and group work

- learning logs.

What are we working on?

It is important that students know what they have to do. This may sound obvious but most teachers just tell pupils. What happens if they are not listening at that moment? What happens if they are absent? So often pupils only have a hazy idea of what they are working on. They can remember what happened in class last week: 'We did a bit about rivers, animals on a farm, and "camping" is the same word in English and French, and Billy Moffat got sent out for throwing things.' That is a far cry from knowing that they are working on structures and vocabulary for holidays!

A simple way to keep track of the curriculum and objectives is to write them down on a piece of paper and pin them up somewhere in the MFL area. A noticeboard could be developed with separate sections for different year groups. Keep referring to it till the objectives are fulfilled. It can be written in pupil friendly language, and have symbols or pictures. If we want to help pupils make real progress and become more independent, we have to share the aims with learners, so they will know what they are aiming for and when they have achieved it. Of course this does not have to be in print – it could be done in symbols, with pictures, or in Braille.

Pair work

Languages are about communication and talking, so why do many schools spend so much time making everyone do their piece of work, quietly and on their own? If ever a subject was made for collaborative pair work, it is language learning. Everyone will have talents – from the child with a good memory who can recall a word others have forgotten, to the child with good dictionary skills who can look up words, to the child who can mimic well and has a limited vocabulary but a good sense of how the language should sound.

Sharing ideas and putting thoughts into words helps students learn. Often it engages problem-solving skills instead of just dealing with, and repeating, received information. If we don't know how to say something in a foreign language we have to develop strategies to get round the problem. These might involve asking someone else, looking it up, or finding things we do know and working out if we can adapt those. These are all real-life strategies which will stand pupils in good stead when they go abroad.

Providing learning logs

There is a fashion now for pupils to record their feelings and evaluate their own learning. Is it worth it? If a pupil just writes 'OK' every time, are we any further forward? Does it serve any purpose other than to add to a mound of paperwork? Some schools work with a line:

1	2	3	4	5	6
bad					good

Pupils circle the number which comes closest to their views. Always have six choices rather than five, otherwise everyone circles number 3! Other schools use words or symbols to speed up the process. One interesting example is given by Jen Taylor in *IT Support for All* (NCET out of print):

> One fairly able student, despite starting work keenly and calmly each lesson, regularly became frustrated to the point of violence when asked to write more

than a few sentences. The teacher got him to put a 'How do you feel?' face at the end of every line, or when he got stuck. They discovered within a couple of lessons that the frustration that was provoking such an outburst was an inability to remember some basic spelling and syntactical rules. They were able to address these through structured teaching and over time he became a confident and successful learner – beginning to understand the triggers to his own anger and thinking about wider solutions.

Think about pupils doing this recording and evaluating in pairs. Pupils may think they have done really badly, but someone else may be able to say, 'Well, the first bit was good when we did about the weather, but then we didn't know any words for sports.' A conversation like this is a far more valuable evaluation than all the bits of paper!

Notes

1 Query on Inclusion website: http://inclusion.ngfl.gov.uk
2 McNamara, S. and Moreton, G. (1997) *Understanding Differentiation – A Teacher's Guide.* London: David Fulton.
3 See www.talkingdice.co.uk/ for details of this product.

CHAPTER 6

Monitoring and Assessment

Why assess?

This may seem a strange question when we work in an era that sometimes seems to be obsessed with measuring pupil competency and pupil progress. Some people argue that assessments are just tests which show what children can't do. They say targets are imposed solely by staff or external bodies which provide standardised scores for league tables. They feel that such assessments generate figures that give no real indication of whether pupils are working to their full potential, and may disadvantage pupils with special needs. However, if we are just going through the motions and seeing assessment as an administrative requirement, we are missing the point.

At a simple level, assessment should check whether pupils have completed work. MFL teachers will need to record progress in all four skill areas (reading, writing, speaking and listening) over a period of time. Regular marking and recording enables teachers to see which units pupils have missed. Although language learning is not linear, pupils often need to acquire one set of skills in order to move on to the next level. Where children have missed a lesson where a grammar point was explained, they may have an incomplete understanding of how the language works. Assessment can point up the gaps in their reasoning.

Assessment provides an ideal opportunity to check whether learning has taken place, to test out the success of teaching methods and to tailor provision to meet the needs of individual pupils. Monitoring and assessment should give not just a set of grades but also promote reflection about what works, which styles of learning predominate in a group and how to remediate or extend limited knowledge. We also need to consider the pupil's own place in the process in terms of self-assessment.

Departmental handbooks are an important starting point for establishing clear procedures and guidance for MFL teachers on assessment matters. The most effective handbooks link assessment, recording and reporting policy for MFL to objectives in the departmental development plan, with analysis of assessment data contributing to annual action plans and directly influencing medium- and long-term planning. For example, teachers use information about pupils' specific strengths and weaknesses well in planning future units and lessons, such as in targeting weak areas of vocabulary or deficiencies in spelling. As recommended in Ofsted's *Good assessment practice in modern foreign languages:*

- They use January Year 9 examinations to identify areas of skill and understanding to raise in National Curriculum levels by the end of Key Stage 3, particularly the level 5 'hurdle' in attainment target 2 and 4;

- They use June Year 10 module results to identify areas for improvement in listening and reading skills.[1]

Formative assessment

When teachers and LSAs start working with a new group, it is important to assess prior knowledge. While reports may be passed on from the previous year, they can be unreliable guides. Some pupils make enormous leaps in their development over the school holidays, while others seem to forget everything they have been taught. It is a good idea to have a settling-in period of a few lessons to recall the language and to practise all four skills before any more formal assessment takes place. Without an assessment, staff, pupils and TAs may have no clear idea of what the pupils can and can't do or of the best ways of helping them to learn. Formative assessment can:

- provide a diagnostic tool

- help staff to identify misconceptions and misunderstandings

- highlight underachievement

- support target-setting and/or monitoring

- help teachers to clarify objectives

- help with future planning

- help teachers to anticipate future problems

- help teachers to develop appropriate challenge

- let the pupil see what they CAN do

- raise expectations – for both staff and pupils

In many ways, the assessment process is cyclical. For example, during a listening comprehension activity about daily routines, the teacher will check that all pupils understand how to express the time in the target language and indeed that they can all tell the time. If problems are identified, the teacher could decide to use warm-up activities on numbers, time and the 24-hour clock at the beginning of the next lesson. In other words, formative assessment needs to inform planning.

Finding out what works and what doesn't

Assessment is not just about remediation or plugging the gaps. Sometimes teachers don't realise that assessment is about their successes and failures too. 'I've taught them about the imperfect and how to use it but hardly any of them got it right in their homework' translates into, 'I've told them but they haven't learnt it.' The wise teacher thinks, 'There must be another way', and sets about finding it. It may be that the imperfect was explained in a way that only worked for the good listeners, and she needs to make adjustments for those who operate on a more visual level. Sometimes using a PowerPoint demonstration on a whiteboard can help those pupils who need extra practice on some features of the target language. Animations and sound effects can bring a topic to life and make it more memorable. The important point here is that when assessment throws up gaps in knowledge across a significant number of pupils, the teacher needs to reconsider strategies.

Teachers need to think about how they use questioning. Is it to improve pronunciation or to check on knowledge of grammar and vocabulary? How might they elicit longer answers? Typical questions which would do so could be pinned on the wall, with examples of short, medium and long answers, e.g.:

'Quel temps fait-il?'

'Il neige' . . . 'Il neige et il fait froid' . . . 'Il neige, il fait froid et le ciel est noir.'

'Je peux vous aider?'

'Je voudrais une chambre' . . . 'Je voudrais une chambre pour deux personnes' . . . 'Je voudrais une chambre pour deux personnes pour trois nuits, du lundi au jeudi.'

Alternatively, give pupils a grid:

Je voudrais une chambre:

Pour . . . nuits	avec	Y-a-t'il . . . ?
Du . . . au	Un grand lit	Un court de tennis
	Douche	Un solarium
	Salle du bain	Un jardin
	Bidet	Une piscine
	Chauffage central	Un restaurant
	Balcon	
	Vue sur mer	

Homework is crucial as it gives pupils time and space to practise and extend their learning as well as providing evidence of achievement. It needs to be followed up in class and seen as an integral part of the learning process and not just as an optional extra. However, the teacher does not necessarily need to see each piece of homework: pupils can mark each other's work in class with appropriate guidance and will often be far tougher on one another than the teacher would be.

You might find that a particular teaching strategy results in exceptionally good learning. Once you find out what works with particular pupils, you can think about how to extend the same methods to other topics. You may need to differentiate assessments. You can test the same points at different levels or in different ways. For an example of this see Appendix 6.1 for testing German vocabulary.

Of course, external examinations come in a prescribed form but you may find that you can better gauge what pupils can do at the end of a unit by devising creative assessments which link more closely to their learning style. Role play, pupil-generated quizzes and dialogues may be effective tests of knowledge and understanding. Gardner's theory of Multiple Intelligences has been very influential in educational circles but is often overlooked in the assessment process. There is an excellent downloadable version of this on the Standards Site in the DfES publication *Learning Styles and Writing in Modern Foreign Languages*.[2] Look at Appendix 6.2 to see an illustration of the different intelligences which most closely link to MFL. There is also an online interactive worksheet which produces a multiple intelligences wheel based upon Gardner's eight multiple intelligences.[3]

Ongoing formal assessment

The National Curriculum Guidance is a good starting point for thinking about assessment. It states that teachers use appropriate assessment approaches when they:

- allow for different learning styles and ensure that pupils are given the chance and encouragement to demonstrate their competence and attainment through appropriate means;

- are familiar to the pupils and for which they have been adequately prepared;

- use materials which are free from discrimination and stereotyping in any form;

- provide clear and unambiguous feedback to pupils to aid further learning.

In order to overcome potential barriers to learning and assessment for individuals and groups of pupils, teachers should set targets for learning that:

- build on pupils' knowledge, experiences, interests and strengths to improve areas of weakness and demonstrate progression over time;

- are attainable and yet challenging and help pupils to develop their self-esteem and confidence in their ability to learn.

P levels

These are for pupils who are working at lower levels of achievement, and offer a useful way of monitoring progression.

P4 Pupils attempt to repeat, copy or imitate some sounds heard in the target language. They may perform familiar or simple actions on request, using repetition, sign or gesture as prompts. They listen and may respond to familiar rhymes and songs in a foreign language.

P5 Pupils attempt one or two words in the target language in response to cues in a song or familiar phrase. They respond to simple questions, requests or instructions about familiar events or experiences. Responses may be through vocalisation, sign or gesture, and pupils' responses may depend upon repetition and support.

P6 Pupils respond to others in a group. Their attempts to communicate in the target language may rely heavily upon repetition and gesture, and they may use facial expression and/or intonation to enhance meaning. They communicate positives and negatives in the target language in response to simple questions. They match and select symbols for familiar words, actions or objects presented in the target language.

P7 Pupils introduce themselves by name in response to a question in the target language. They contribute to using the target language for a purpose, for example using ICT skills to access the Internet and exchange information, with guidance from other pupils or adults. They listen, attend to and follow familiar interactions in the target language.

P8 Pupils listen attentively and know that the target language conveys meaning. They understand one or two simple classroom commands in the target language. They respond briefly using single words, signs or symbols. They may need considerable support from a spoken model and from visual clues. They may read and understand a few words presented in a familiar context with visual clues. They can copy out a few words with support. They label one or two objects. With some support, they use the target language for a purpose, for example requesting items in simulations of real life encounters in the target language.

Myles Pilling (as part of his work with mPowernet) has developed a Word Macro to automatically insert the P levels into a Word document.[4]

The level descriptors for MFL are also helpful in giving a structure for measuring progress.

Level descriptions

Level	AT 1	AT 2	AT3	AT4
	Listening – You should be able to:	**Speaking –** You should be able to:	**Reading –** You should be able to:	**Writing –** You should be able to:
1	Understand a word	Say a word or phrase	Read a word	Copy down a word
2	Understand a sentence or question	Say a sentence	Read a sentence/ use a dictionary	Copy down a sentence. Write words from memory
3	Understand a short conversation	Say two or three things in a conversation	Read a conversation. Read a text	Write two or three sentences using book to help. Write down a sentence from memory
4	Understand a longer conversation	Say three or four things in a conversation	Read a short story. Work out what something means	Write four sentences from memory

Ongoing informal assessment

Not all assessment has to be in the form of a test. Some teachers use focused observation. This gives them a chance to evaluate strengths and weaknesses. If the class is working in small groups, it is an ideal time to check out such matters as turn taking, who is silent, who lacks concentration, who opts out, which pupils perform better in groups rather than whole-class situations, who has a good accent, who needs help with pronunciation, whether there are any signs of bullying, etc. It may also be a good time to check on particular points on IEPs. If a pupil is working on listening skills or behavioural targets, these can be observed too.

Cloze is a good way of assessing whether learning has taken place. Often it is hard to establish what pupils know if they have problems with speaking or writing. A cloze passage enables them to fill in the gaps without getting bogged down in explanations or being held back by poor articulation or slow handwriting.

The example on page 83 was made using *ClozePro* from Crick software.

Feedback to pupils

Apart from question and answer activities in class, marking is the most obvious form of feedback. Drill and practice computer programs are particularly effective in this context because they provide speedy individualised responses in a way that a teacher in a class of 30 pupils cannot. They can check a response, urge a pupil to try again if they have chosen an incorrect answer, provide explanations and offer rewards in the form of sound effects, animations or even printed certificates on successful completion of tasks. However, they only work well for certain forms of learning and for developing particular skills. They can help with grammar, vocabulary and spelling where accuracy is paramount but they are not suitable for more creative tasks. Drill and practice software is good for motivating some pupils and has a lot to offer to learners who have a short attention span or who need considerable over-learning in order to retain particular structures.

Drill and practice activities are a good form of testing and the better programs keep a record of pupil responses so teachers can see how many attempts a pupil made before getting a right answer. In practice, this information is sometimes so detailed that a teacher needs a considerable amount of time to track each pupil.

Teacher marking needs to be prompt and in a form that the pupils can understand. Although it is good to put comments in the target language, some pupils working at P levels would not understand the difference between 'très bien' and 'assez bien'. A system of different coloured stickers may make the point more effectively. Some teachers like to divide marks to record effort and result so pupils see that it is worth trying harder and that this will be rewarded, but pupils need a clear understanding of the difference between effort and attainment.

Marking should be as detailed as possible. The teacher needs to pick out errors and show how to improve accuracy (e.g. position of adjectives, gender, use of capitals/lower case, etc.). Pupils need to be set targets and shown what they need to do to improve. The teacher also needs to provide oral feedback to the individual and/or to the class, making teaching points out of the more common mistakes. This is for the benefit of those who do not necessarily obtain information from text.

File Edit View Session Report Options Help

Spel Check Remove Text Replace Text Remove Words Add Cell Remove Cell Activity Settings Notes Run

B *I* U

Primero, visitaremos la Plaza de España y _____ un aperitivo o cerveza en El Pintor Blanco, _____ bar. Luego cenaremos en un restaurante _____ estilo buffet antes de _____ un espectáculo de flamenco. En la misma zona, Estrillo _____ una aldea de pescadores, perfecta para un _____ de descanso. Sin _____, las playas en esta parte _____ muy lindas! El _____ está a través de un _____ en el bosque. Playa Numa es la playa _____ próxima del Centro donde se _____ bañar.

son	es	más	sendero
día	típico	disfrutar	acceso
puede	duda	famoso	tomaremos

An example of a cloze passage designed with Crick software

Pupils know what to do

Effective assessment involves constant monitoring and feedback to pupils and appropriate action to promote improvement, as in the following example:

> The teacher picks up points to correct in plenary, and does so rigorously and sensitively, getting the class to repeat the correct answers so that all can benefit without individual pupils being demoralised. She gives credit for an 'almost right' answer, but doesn't stop there. She commends pupils who take the initiative in going beyond the minimum with an extended utterance, in order to raise the expectations of the rest. In monitoring oral work in pairs, she explains how the utterance can be improved, using reference to similar patterns or to work covered earlier. She makes it clear how pupils can get better at reading the target language by linking a comment to the national curriculum levels which are displayed in the classroom for all to see. (Ofsted HM1 1478)

Pupils tend to find it easier to identify their progress in written than in oral work, but oral work does have one advantage in that it offers the possibility of quick feedback. In general, their awareness of how well they are doing is linked to the amount of effort invested by teachers into explaining criteria and systems. For example, in the report quoted above, Ofsted commented:

> 'Pupils were made well aware of how they were doing in speaking during "routine" oral work, and by periodic mini-tests in speaking, which they had to re-do until they got a satisfactory mark. They were alerted to the most common errors in writing as these were discussed by the teachers with the whole class. In another school, pupils could explain what was expected in terms of the school's content – language accuracy mark scheme – and were provided with very clear information about effort grades, homework marking; national curriculum level descriptions and examination criteria.'

Tell them, show them, work with them so they have a clear idea of what sort of work they should produce. Again be explicit.

> Tu es en vacances avec ta famille. Écris une carte postale (environ 30 mots) à ton correspondant canadien/ta correspondante canadienne.
>
> Où es-tu? (la ville ou la région)
> Que fais-tu? (du sport? des visites? etc.)
> Quel temps fait-il? (froid? beau? etc.)
> Quand tu rentres en Angleterre?

Pupils need to know exactly what is required:

- I want you to write between 25 and 40 words.

- You must put something for each of the questions.

- There must be a greeting such as 'Salut'.

- There must be a goodbye phrase such as 'A bientôt' to show you have finished.

- You must sign it.

If a pupil's answer is not quite right, you could talk to them about it but they might not take it in. You could ask them to do it again but it might be no better. Instead, find a pupil's work which is that little bit better than theirs and get them to tell you where the difference lies. It might be an idea to photocopy some of the strongest responses for use in this way (possibly erasing the pupil's name). An answer might be, for example, 'She put more about what they did on holiday.' If you show pupils the best work in the class, it is too far ahead of where the less able pupils are so they will switch off. Find work which is the next stage up from theirs. It also gives a boost to the child whose work is chosen. Work together with the child or pair them up with another pupil to bring their work up a notch.

Self-assessment plays an important role in helping pupils to understand assessment objectives and criteria, as in the following example:

'"Aim High" sheets set out for each skill the national curriculum level descriptions presented in 'pupil-friendly' language. Pupils use these to monitor their progress and to identify what they need to do to reach a higher level in a particular skill. They find this motivating and, along with other strategies, such as pupil tracking, it has resulted in pupils' performance in MFL rising significantly in recent years.' (Ofsted HM1 1478)

In effective MFL departments, recording and analysis of assessment information are complemented by focused target setting. Targets are included in reports and discussed during parent/pupil interviews. The same report, for example, states:

'GCSE grades are estimated at three points in Key Stage 4: December of Year 10, end of Year 10, after Year 11 mocks. On each occasion these are shared and discussed with pupils in "off timetable" individual interviews. Another school sets interim learning targets, such as "learn the spelling of these ten words" as opposed to "improve your spelling" which is too general. Each pupil has a summary sheet on which he/she must enter "what I have done about this". The teacher signs off each target when it is achieved.'

Individual Action Plans

One secondary school has developed a modular curriculum across Key Stage 3. All modules run for half a term and have their own course booklet stating the overall aims, as well as containing some of the learning resources, activities and evaluation materials. They then have a menu of objectives, perhaps a dozen. During the first lesson of the new half term in each subject, pupils negotiate with the teacher, identifying five or six appropriate targets from the list, for example:

Je dois appendre:

Les jours	Les sports
Les mois	Les nombres jusqu' à vingt
Les passetemps	Les animaux

Each pupil has a personal organiser and these targets are recorded so that they can be shared with parents and referred to both at school and when doing homework. Pupils, parents and teachers are delighted with the system, and are finding that even the youngest pupils are taking much more responsibility for their learning and taking a pride in their achievements. It has also helped tremendously with individual learning plans for pupils with special educational needs where the vast majority of the paperwork is now neatly contained in the pupils' personal organiser and teachers' regular class records, in just the same format as everyone else's. In a sense it means that for French, everyone has an IEP instead of just 'special' pupils.

A school in Nottingham has Bull's Eye sheets. Pupils write three targets they want to achieve – learn to count to 50, learn words for rooms in the house, learn how to say what I would like to eat. They work out how this will happen. Will they put the numbers on a tape, will they sing them, recite them to a friend or their Dad? How many numbers will they know by next week? How many the week after? The whole point is that they set the goals and work out how they will know if they are getting there.

External examinations

Pupils need practice in taking examinations. The first step, however, is to identify which examination is appropriate. If you are teaching modern foreign languages to students who are low achievers, or you need some kind of award to mark progress in French, Spanish or German, then alternatives to GCSE should be considered. Indeed, QCA recommend that you do so:

> Schools will need to explore the full range of accredited language courses at Key Stage 4, including vocational options, to offer language learning through a more diverse range of courses and curriculum contexts, to suit individual pupil needs and aspirations and enhance future employability.[5]

Alternatives to GCSE such as the Certificate of Achievement or GNVQ Key Stage 4 language units provide genuine opportunities for pupils to achieve success within a national examination framework. More details can be found in Appendix 6.3. Alternatives to GCSE/GCE are being considered because:

- in 2004 the study of a modern foreign language at Key Stage 4 will become an entitlement rather than a requirement;

- take up of post-16 languages is low and has declined in most languages over the past decade;

- students throughout the phase will be following programmes that are more individual and include different vocational qualifications.

Popular alternatives include the Secondary Certificate in Language Learning from Birmingham Advisory and Support Service or the Entry level qualifications from WJEC.

For the Secondary Certificate in Language Learning, pupils have to complete seven modules from a choice of ten, including two compulsory ones which are used for moderation. The scheme covers all four skills and is pitched at levels 1–3 so it can be used as an alternative, or as a staging post for GCSE. It is topic-based and is compatible with all major courses. All the assessment materials are supplied and a dedicated course book is available.[6]

The WJEC specification is broadly targeted at those who have not reached level 3 of the National Curriculum at the end of their study of a modern foreign language at Key Stage 3. This specification is designed for those pupils in the 14+ age group who would not, at the outset of the course, be expected to attain a grade G at GCSE. There is no summative examination.

Examination of pupils' achievement in the attainment targets is made under controlled conditions by discrete continuous testing of set tasks during each of ten units of work. This is carried out on a half-termly basis between the autumn term of Year 10 and the summer term of Year 11. Unit 1 forms the compulsory moderation core, to be set and moderated during the autumn term of Year 10. Of the remaining nine units, WJEC recommends that centres teach the units in the order in which they appear in the syllabus. The tests generate marks that provide evidence of pupils' attainment.

For details of the WJEC specification and a range of alternative qualifications see Appendix 6.3.

Accommodating the needs of pupils with SEN

Once you have decided on an appropriate qualification, think about whether special arrangements will be necessary for individual pupils. Examination boards are bound by SENDA and will be covered by Part IV of the Act. This means that candidates cannot be treated less favourably on the grounds of their disability in an exam setting. Exam boards are generally quite helpful about the special requirements for particular pupils to show their achievements.

The Joint Council for General Qualification issues guidance to exam boards and to centres.

Summary of principles for centres

The centre should:

- 7.1 choose the qualification or the option(s) within a qualification which is most appropriate for the candidate with a known long-term or permanent disability or learning difficulty. The requirements of the candidate and the implications for the assessment should be considered when he/she applies for a course;

- 7.2 recognise the requirements of each candidate individually making use of specialist advice from external sources, as appropriate;

- 7.3 ensure that all applications for special arrangements and special consideration are supported by the Head of Centre and are submitted no later than the due dates;

- 7.4 ensure that the arrangements requested will assist the candidate to demonstrate his/her attainment without affecting or circumventing assessment requirements;

- 7.5 consider the candidate's normal way of learning and producing work as a basis for special arrangements provided that this would not give the candidate an unfair advantage or compromise the integrity of the examination or assessment;

- 7.6 ensure that the candidate has experience of and practice in the use of the arrangements requested.

Schools need to ensure that:

- special assessment arrangements do not give unfair advantage over other candidates;

- arrangements are determined according to the particular disability or learning difficulty;

- users of certificates are not misled about candidate attainment.

The arrangements may include extra time, additional facilities or some level of support, for example pupils with a physical disability may be allowed a writer, extra time allowance (normally 25%) and mechanical/electronic aids. Students with a visual impairment may have a writer, a reader, tapes, question papers with large print, Braille or Moon, use of a keyboard to produce typescript answers or raised type responses to a question paper, extra time allowance (normally 25%) and mechanical/electronic equipment.

Awarding bodies will not provide enlarged question papers for candidates with such difficulties, but centres may, with the permission of the awarding body, open question papers up to one hour prior to the examination in order to make enlargements or photocopy onto coloured paper. Centres must take responsibility for ensuring that the entire paper is copied and for maintaining the security of the question paper.

Arrangements for pupils with a hearing impairment may include the use of a communicator/interpreter, extra time allowance (normally 25%) and mechanical/electronic aids. Signing of questions or the oral presentation of questions using the oral/aural approach may be permitted for candidates with a hearing impairment (except where reading is an assessment objective) in exceptional circumstances, if either approach is the usual method of communication in the classroom and access to the examination cannot be achieved by other means. Special amplification for aural tests may be permitted for hearing-impaired candidates. Reading of the tests to enable candidates to lip-read may also be permitted. In addition, candidates whose hearing loss results in a possible linguistic disability may be provided with question papers with appropriate modified wording, as recommended by a specialist teacher of the deaf.

In the case of candidates with specific learning difficulties of a dyslexic or similar nature, arrangements may include a writer and/or a reader, extra time allowance (normally 25%), tapes and typescripts of answers, and coloured overlays/paper. Some visual difficulties are normally corrected by the use of tinted spectacles or coloured overlays, and permission for the use of these aids does not have to be sought from the awarding body. Arrangements for candidates with other learning difficulties may include a writer and/or a reader, extra time allowance (normally 25%) and other audio/visual aids as appropriate to the needs of the individual.

Notes

1 *Good assessment practice in modern foreign languages.* Ofsted HMI 1478. Document on website: http://www.slamnet.org.uk/mfl/MFL.doc
2 DfES 0382/2002, available on website: www.standards.dfes.gov.uk
3 This is available on the Birmingham Grid for Learning website: www.bgfl.org/Use the search facility.
4 See: http://www.argonet.co.uk/users/richard.walter/schem.html
5 DfES (2002) *Languages for all: languages for life.*
6 The coursebook can be obtained from: Martineau Centre, Balden Road, Harborne, Birmingham B32 2EH Tel: 0121 303 8146.

CHAPTER 7

Managing Support

Support staff numbers now stand at over 216,000 (full-time equivalent) in the 23,000 schools in England. The Government's recent and planned investment means that, during this Parliament alone, support staff numbers will have grown by at least 50,000.[1]

All Teaching Assistants, whether they are foreign language assistants or are employed to help pupils with special needs, need to be managed well and their role must be clear. This chapter will look at their work in relation to:

- helping with the care and support of individual pupils

- helping with the care and support of a group of pupils

- supporting learning activities

- assisting with classroom resources and records

Compare these scenarios:

> Tom is a Learning Assistant in a Year 8 German class. He supports Malik who has Retinitis Pigmentosa and has very little peripheral vision. Tom does not speak German. He and Malik sit at the back of the class and, when the German class is engaged in reading and writing activities, Tom spends the time testing Malik on his spellings for English or helping him catch up with his homework for other subjects.

> Kuldip has severe learning difficulties. He is in Year 7, finds it hard to cope with the changes of lessons and is reluctant to speak in class. Myra, his TA, has collected some items for his German box. This contains a picture book about Germany, a small map, a picture of the Bayern Munich football team and a Walkman with a tape of German greetings. She opens the box at the start of the lesson to help him get oriented. He sees the objects and it helps him to focus on German and call to mind some of the words he knows so he has a context for learning. The class is working on *Zu Hause*. Although Myra has only been learning German alongside the class, she has copied some core vocabulary and structures from the worksheets onto a Clicker Grid so Kuldip can build up a piece of writing and print it.

Alison has a good relationship with Billy who has learning difficulties and some behavioural problems. She takes a keen interest in his welfare and if he is unhappy, he often seeks her out at lunchtime in the Base. She has made a real difference to his confidence but she is over-protective. She often praises him when he has made very little effort. There are also issues about how much of the work is his. The final straw was when the children had to draw their bedroom and then label the furniture in German for homework. Billy's work was really good, especially considering he was absent!

What does an assistant do?

Support staff may be called by different names in different authorities. They may be called Teaching Assistants (TAs), Special Support Assistants, Pupil Assistants, Statement Support Assistants or Learning Support Assistants (LSAs). Their role is to help teachers and to work with other professionals such as speech and language therapists and parents to support children's learning. Some are allocated to an individual pupil with special needs, while others support a whole class or groups within the class. Support staff may also provide administrative support, technical support, or be involved in pastoral care.

While TAs do not 'teach', their input is crucial to successful teaching, and their observations inform the short- and long-term planning for individuals and whole classes. Sometimes teachers and TAs work together with experts, for example with advisory teachers, educational psychologists or speech and language therapists, to plan programmes for the pupil. Targets from these programmes can be incorporated into Individual Education Plans (IEPs).

In April 2003 there was a particularly lively discussion on Senco-forum about the variety of ways in which ancillary staff were used in schools. One school has two different categories of TA:

- Some TAs are used for general classroom support and are involved in:
  - photocopying
  - displays
  - helping with administration
  - collecting money
  - first aid (those who have done the training)
  - playground supervision
  - being 'an extra adult' in the classroom to support as and when needed (often working with the least able or the most able to supervise differentiated group work)

- Other TAs, specifically attached to pupils who have special needs (as statemented provision)
  - work 1:1 or support a small group which includes that child
  - help with preparation of materials
  - support organisation and inclusion strategies

– deal with specific physio, speech and language or dyspraxia programmes and IEP targets

– carry out observations and keep records of progress

Other schools have different models:

> We have SEN TAs, one for each year group, who support individual children and groups. We also have one general TA per class who supports children, but also does lots of organisational stuff (tidying, pencil sharpening and photocopying etc.). We always write these types of things into the job description, because somebody has to do it or the class/group doesn't function. Usually TA and teacher share tasks.[2]

Helping with the care and support of individual pupils

Undoubtedly, some of the pupils would not access the curriculum or make the progress that they do without the expertise and encouragement that is provided by TAs. The TA will perform a variety of roles including acting as a scribe, simplifying instructions, providing key words, in the case of visual impairment making sure text is enlarged, and in all cases helping the pupil to achieve the targets in the IEP.

There are various ways of providing individualised support. The TA is in an ideal position to bolster up the pupil in a way that the class teacher does not have time to do. Ideally, the TA should:

- take an interest in the pupil's interests

- notice when he or she is feeling low

- give support when needed

- encourage effort

- develop listening skills

- inspire confidence and trust

- have positive expectations

One of the central questions is: should TAs only work with the designated child? The answer to this will usually be 'No'. Some children with special needs don't like being singled out as the one needing extra help and sometimes the TA can effectively exclude the pupil as in the following example:

Nuala has severe hearing loss. Her LEA has recently provided an audio typist to sit at her side and type what is said in class. Nuala reads this off a screen and so keeps pace with the rest of the group. However, this means that Nuala cannot choose where she sits in class or who she sits next to. She is welded to her typist. This is her main form of communication with the class. While everyone is looking and listening, her eyes are fixed on the screen and she misses a lot of the interaction. The school needs to reassess what her needs are and find a way of integrating her more fully in the class and meeting her communications needs.

In his book, *Reaching Out to All Learners*[3], Mel Ainscow reports that:

In general, our impression was that whilst these pupils seen as having special needs were following broadly the same activities as their classmates, the constant presence of a 'helper' meant that often the challenges posed by these activities were significantly reduced.

Even in these days when the term 'inclusion' is quite widely understood, there is still a real danger of walking into a classroom and seeing a child with Down's Syndrome or a pupil with a visual impairment sitting in a different part of the room doing different tasks. This cannot be justified as differentiation!

There is also an issue about making the best use of the TA's time. What if the class is watching a video? Does the TA need to be there? What if they are engaged in pair work? Does three become a crowd? What if the child is ill, does the TA get paid? There are also issues of dependence. It is true that children needing specialist equipment get fed up with 'breaking in' new Learning Assistants and find it easier to work with someone who knows how the kit works and how best to help them. On the other hand, if that TA is ill or leaves, the child can feel bereft. One-to-one support is fraught with dangers. There is a school of thought which runs along these lines:

Kerry's speech is hard to understand and she seems very happy working with Mel. Mel knows what she's doing so I let her get on with it. This gives me more time to work with others who need help.

In this case, Kerry might just as well be in another class.

You may want the TA to concentrate on one child but supplement this with keeping an eye on other children in the class who are falling behind or need extra stimulation. This can be tricky if the TA insists that the job description specifies supporting one individual. It might be worth pointing out that no child works in isolation and part of the TA's role is to ensure an inclusive setting which cannot be achieved by isolating the child and smothering him/her with one-to-one attention.

The teacher's role is to teach and to make sure that there are activities which are within the grasp of all the pupils in the classroom. Where there is a good relationship with a TA planning does become a joint enterprise. The good TA is always aware that the individual is also part of a group and will do everything to foster good relations between pupils.

Helping with the care and support of a group of pupils

Many TAs find they are supporting a group of low achievers, rather than one named child. Again there is a danger of dividing the class into subsets. Many of us have seen classrooms where there is an obvious 'remedial table'. If a group of the more challenging children are sitting together under the direction of the TA, they are being segregated, not included. This approach also sets up problems in the long term because children:

- become dependent on the TA and will not get on with work if left unsupervised;

- develop irritating behavioural ticks learnt from each other through peer modelling;

- have low self-esteem because they are 'in the thickies group';

- fail to benefit from working with pupils who have different strengths and weaknesses;

- receive too little direct teaching from the class teacher because the TA is in attendance;

- are not set sufficiently challenging tasks.

Working with groups of pupils means that there are obvious time savings but there may be a danger that the quieter pupils miss out because the louder ones demand attention. Guidelines for working with learners in the MFL classroom are in Appendix 7.1.

It is more effective to pinpoint individuals who will benefit from extra support and to specify what that support might be. It is the teacher's job to decide how the lessons will proceed and what styles of teaching are appropriate. Where possible, the teacher should provide the TA with a lesson plan with notes about individual pupils. This can be very simple as in this example of a lesson, based on checking and reinforcing French town vocabulary:

Teacher	Pupils	Notes to TA
Hold up pictures.	Call out vocabulary.	Tom at front please.
Distribute scissors + vocabulary sheet *Chez Moi.*	Cut up to make flash cards.	
		Enlarged pictures for Tom. Watch Louise with scissors. Shannon will need help cutting. Don't let Arun and Kyle sit together.
Check understanding, answer questions.	Draw pictures.	Check all five on task; get Shannon to draw at least four!!

As well as working alongside the teacher in class, the TA may also withdraw pupils for some specialist support. They may work one to one: helping with problem solving, providing pastoral support, giving active listening, or catching up with work. Alternatively, there may be small groups focusing on social skills, problem solving or anger management, and the timetabling for this should be negotiated between the SENCO and subject teachers.

Where teacher and TA are working together in a class, there needs to be a consistent approach. They need to share the same philosophy and agree classroom management:

It took time for classroom culture to change to the extent that the second adult felt free to move around while the lead teacher was delivering the substance of the lesson. There were also potential tensions when adolescents inevitably tested the boundaries. It was important that the support teacher was able to sit calmly in the classroom and read unspoken signals from the lead teacher. Both teachers needed to have a will to make working together effective for the children, even if sometimes it meant hiding feelings and deferring to each other. (Lovey 2002:7)[4]

Supporting learning activities

Apart from specific care for individual pupils, TAs can provide general support for study skills. This might include:

- producing a visual timetable

- checking the pupil has the right equipment for lessons – pens, coloured pencils, rulers, dictionary, etc.

- dealing with mounds of bits of paper which collect in bag/folders and helping the pupil to be organised

- providing extra practice for spellings

- reinforcing key vocabulary

- showing them how to set out work neatly

- keeping a check on homework – especially if child is not going to get support at home

- help with structuring revision

TAs may need to learn how particular resources help particular pupils. For instance, there are various MFL computer-assisted learning packages with exercises and listening practice and they may need to learn how to use these programs.

Sometimes, their role grows and expands to encompass a whole new approach as in this example:

Brakenhale is a community comprehensive school for 11–18 year olds. Of the 633 students, 46% are on the school's special needs register and 17 have statements – over half these statements include emotional and behavioural difficulties and moderate learning difficulties. There is a high turnover of staff and the school has had particular difficulties with children with learning and behavioural problems.

TAs, however, are not given a hard time by the vast majority of pupils because they are seen as allies and friends. TAs are helpful negotiators with the pupils. According to the SENCO:

- We have evidence that the TAs do much good for the pupils.

- We can evidence improved attendance.

- We can show increases in reading age measures.

- The TAs can identify the pupils who are not coping, often better than teachers who have other concerns to address.

- The TAs have improved the social skills of youngsters.

- 'Sort and support' pupils show real improvement.

Often the TAs swap roles with teachers, with the TA managing the whole class while the teacher deals with individuals. The TAs also work with the newly established homework club and provide the total supervision for five nights per week.[5]

Assisting with classroom resources and records

TAs may be employed to assist with paperwork, filing and resource management, and consequently reduce teacher workloads. In the future, there is likely to be more administrative support in schools. The DfES circular 2/98 *Reducing the Bureaucratic Burden on Teachers* lists 24 non-teaching tasks which teachers routinely perform and proposes that many of these should be undertaken by support staff so that teachers can focus more closely on teaching. Such tasks include:

- collecting money
- chasing absences
- bulk photocopying
- copy typing
- producing standard letters
- producing class lists
- record keeping and filing
- making classroom displays
- analysing attendance figures
- processing exam results
- collating pupil reports
- administering work experience
- administering examinations
- administering teacher cover
- ICT trouble shooting and minor repairs
- commissioning new ICT equipment
- ordering supplies and equipment
- stocktaking
- cataloguing, preparing, issuing and maintaining equipment and materials
- minuting meetings
- co-ordinating and submitting bids
- seeking and giving personnel advice
- managing pupil data
- inputting pupil data

Many of these tasks apply particularly to the MFL classroom. Teachers will welcome offers to help organise a trip to France, to collect money and make arrangements with the coach company etc., or to prepare letters to be sent home. The TA can work with staff and pupils to produce relevant lively wall displays, find out about new materials and programs, do stocktaking and cataloguing of books, worksheets, magazines, realia such as menus, games, cassettes, etc. and in this way get to know more about the subject and how to tailor resources to pupils' needs. In order for this to happen, senior management will have to change the contracts and contact hours for TAs or look at changing their conditions of service. However, if the MFL department puts forward a proposal and shows exactly how and why they would use these additional hours, they are more likely to get a favourable response. If a TA has been appointed to support one pupil who is then absent for a long time, this might be a way to make good use of the TA's time and would provide real long-term benefits for all the MFL staff.

As well as carrying out administrative tasks, the TA may generate additional classroom resources as in the following example:

I used box filing cards, colour coded according to difficulty. When teaching mixed-ability groups for MFL, a box of cards was prepared for each module of the course. These were laminated so they could be taken home for homework. While giving out homework I knew by the colour at a glance which card to give. Each card was numbered so that there was a variety of activities at each level that would consolidate the learning according to the student's ability. If it was a listening exercise, the tape would have a sticker of the same colour with the corresponding card number on it. The cards were often used in class and cassette recorders were available for students to record their sentences privately until they were satisfied. (Lovey 2002:54)[6]

The child with a visual impairment will need additional resources and the RNIB offers this warning:

When you are planning your classroom sessions, ensure that you liaise with the visually impaired child's support assistant or support teacher to advise them of any resources you intend to use. The amount of work needed to adapt resources into large print or Braille can be very time-consuming, particularly in language teaching, where many of the standard resources are very visual, with heavy reliance on cartoons, cursive script and busy pictures.

So try not to change your mind at the last minute! If you are only likely to use two pages of a four-page worksheet, tell the support worker: they will appreciate not having to adapt those extra two pages! And give them ample time to produce resources in modified formats – it will be appreciated and will benefit you when your lessons are far more accessible for your pupil with sight problems![7]

Barriers to success

Communication is vital for harmonious working relationships in any department but there are particular issues within the MFL department. Many TAs do not speak a foreign language, or at least, have no confidence in their ability. While most support staff will happily have a go at history or maths or science, even though they are not experts in that area, they worry about their own skills in French or German. This can have a 'knock-on' effect. They may feel that they are no use and so arrange to support other children at that time in different classes. The 'I'm no good at languages' mentality may spread to the pupils who think, 'Well, if Mrs Clark can't do French, there's no point me trying.' In some schools, they get round this problem by allocating TAs to a particular subject or faculty but you are not necessarily going to find a TA who is good at several languages. One of the obvious strengths of using a TA in the MFL department who has no second language, however, is that they see the lesson through the pupil's eyes. Invariably, this means that such a TA can provide useful feedback to the teacher.

MFL staff must ensure that the ethos of the department is obvious. TAs should be encouraged to take as active a role in languages as they would do in other subjects. Indeed, teachers should work hard to promote the notion that language classes are lively and fun. It is hard to engage and motivate staff who feel they are just carrying out 'dogsbody' duties or are just child-minding.

Different ways of allocating time

Schools have evolved different ways of using TA time. Sometimes the Head of Department is given a number of hours and has to decide how to use them most effectively to support the greatest number of pupils. In some schools, departments have to 'bid' for TA time; in others there are 'specialist' TAs for specific departments. Some schools use a different model and attach a group of TAs to a year group. The TAs come to know the children quite well as they support them in different areas of the curriculum and know something of their strengths and weaknesses, their preferred learning styles, what pressures they face and what triggers bad behaviour. They develop quite a close bond with the pupils and find strategies for encouraging them and keeping them on task. These qualities are more use to a class teacher than someone who can speak French.

Whatever model is used, it is worth noting that staffing tends to be more generous with departments who use TAs 'properly'. If the MFL department has a policy and can show that it uses TAs effectively and values them appropriately, they are more likely to receive a decent allocation of TA time. It is a good idea to consider some of the issues before term starts and discuss how the relationship between teacher and support staff will work. A review sheet is included as Appendix 7.2.

Support and guidance

Again, communication is the key to success. Ask the TAs what support and guidance they might need. Explain that if an activity seems to be pitched at the wrong level and the pupil is finding it too easy or too difficult, their role is to help in differentiation – this may mean:

- simplifying instructions, oral and written
- adapting worksheets to make them easier to understand
- presenting work in short 'chunks'
- providing key words
- developing extension activities

Remind them that their role is to find ways of increasing independence and allowing the pupils to show what they can do. It will not be necessary for them to work alongside a pupil at all times in all lessons; and under no circumstances should they do the work for a pupil. These might be their key duties and responsibilities:

- deal with equipment – specialist equipment and ICT
- observe and record – the participation of individuals during group or class work
- support group work – with objectives set by teacher
- support individual – with care needs
- support individual – with specific task set by teacher
- support individual – with behavioural needs
- administration – carry out administrative tasks set by teacher
- display – take charge of display work
- training – attend relevant training sessions

What if it goes wrong?

Sometimes, with the best will in the world, there is conflict between a teacher and the TA. You will find guidance in any number of management books about how to get the best from staff and deal with grievances but here are some strategies which have been used successfully in schools.

Deal with dissatisfaction FAST. If a TA asks to speak to you, make time as soon as possible. Similarly, if you are unhappy about something, deal with it quickly. Things rarely improve if left unattended.

People may have legitimate grievances so it is important to listen and to keep an open mind. Listen to the content rather than the style of delivery and be aware that they may feel undervalued or unappreciated. Perhaps they have issues in their home life which are spilling over into the work place, making them hard to deal with. You are not a counsellor. You can listen but you can only deal with the things which are in your power. You should not let yourself be caught up too much in personal issues.

Sometimes a very good TA can be a bit too motherly (this does apply to both sexes) and always knows best: 'Oh no I don't think Lawrence would like that. He wouldn't be able to cope.' In some cases, the TA may be scared of stepping out of routine and trying something new; in other cases, they have a need to control everything which relates to 'their pupil'. This may be the time to talk to senior management about your fears that Lawrence is becoming too dependent and that it might be a good idea to foster a new relationship with another TA.

Here are some suggestions for dealing with more confrontational issues:

- Never discuss contentious issues in front of pupils. They gossip and exaggerate.

- Never say anything unpleasant about the TA. It could be slander but in any case it is unprofessional and sours working relationships.

- Remember, nothing in the workplace is really 'off the record'.

- Acknowledge that there is a problem. This can cut the confrontation down to size. By showing the other person that you recognize she is upset (even if the anger seems disproportionate), you are showing you take her seriously.

- Repeat back what has been said. When people hear their own words, they may be caught off guard by the reality of what they have said and may have to rethink it. You are also buying thinking time.

- Reword what the person has said: 'So, what you're really saying is . . .' This causes her to reflect on the implications of what she has said or how she has said it.

- Summarise the discussion. When people are upset, they use a lot of words. Summarising means that you take out the rage and hurt and look at the real issue.

- Ask questions if you feel you are being dragged into an emotional minefield. For example, if a difficult person accuses you of something ludicrous, ask, in a non-threatening way, 'What are you trying to tell me?'

- Defer the discussion to another time in the near future if you cannot deal with it there and then or feel that emotion has overcome reason.

- If the conflict involves a third party, as it so often does, get them together in the same room. It is tempting to see them separately especially if tempers are frayed, but it is better if you can deal with it in an open forum so you cannot be accused of taking sides or talking behind people's backs.

This may sound daunting but in reality, it is very rare to find conflict between teaching staff and TAs that cannot be solved. There are further guidelines in Appendix 7.3 to help you think about your own practice and to ensure that channels of communication are used effectively.

Notes

1 DfES (2002) *Time for Standards.* London: HMSO.
2 Senco-forum, April 2002.
3 Ainscow, M. (1998) *Reaching Out to All Learners.*
4 Lovey, J. (2002) *Supporting Special Educational Needs in Secondary School Classrooms.* London: David Fulton Publishers.
5 Case study from: http://www.teachernet.gov.uk/management/teachingassistants/ Management/casestudies/
6 Op. cit. Lovey
7 *Curriculum Close Up*, the RNIB Curriculum Information Service (01905 357635).

Appendices

Issues for MFL and SEN

Choose two or three of these statements to discuss in team meetings:

It would be very dangerous to take some of our SEN kids abroad. If anything went wrong we could be charged with negligence.

I want to be able to cater for pupils with SEN and would find it beneficial to work with an expert in SEN.

Children with more severe problems will get no benefit from learning a language and will just hold other children back.

Statemented children are the SENCO's responsibility and should be concentrating on basic skills instead of learning a language.

I don't fancy taking kids with behavioural difficulties on the trip to Calais but under the new legislation they have as much right to go as anyone else.

Pupils with special needs have the right to learn a language. They are just as likely to travel as anyone else.

If their behaviour distracts other pupils in any way, youngsters with SEN should be withdrawn from the class.

If my own child had special needs, I would want her/him to learn a foreign language.

Children need to learn about Europe. They are all part of Europe and can't be Little Englanders any more. We need to develop a proper curriculum that is not just a language but covers such topics as culture, history and food.

I need much more time to plan if pupils with SEN are going to be coming to my lessons.

Big schools are just not the right places for blind or deaf kids, or those in wheelchairs.

I have enough to do without worrying about kids who can't read or write.

We should be teaching language awareness – give them a taste of four or five languages instead of doing one in depth.

MFL: Draft Policy for SEN

In the MFL department we will try our best to meet the needs of all pupils so that each and every pupil will have the opportunity to learn a foreign language. We will adapt schemes of work to take account of differing abilities and learning styles.

Management

Pupils will be taught in sets, initially based on KS2 results and information from the primary feeder school. The lower sets will have smaller numbers to allow for more individual attention.

Pupil progress in languages will be reviewed on a regular basis and regular assessment will ensure that pupils are in the right group and that their needs are being met.

There will be differentiated assessment tasks for all pupils at the end of each Module to take account of the full range of abilities.

Targets will be set for individuals and groups on a regular basis. Pupils must know and understand what these targets are and what they have to do to achieve them. Write them in their books if necessary.

Teaching and resources

There will be a variety of approaches to accommodate different learning styles.

A communicative approach will be the main focus of teaching and learning. There will be less emphasis on reading and writing and more on speaking and listening skills.

Visual resources, e.g. flashcards, mime, classroom displays and OHTs will be widely used and built into lesson planning, etc.

A range of reading and writing materials will be provided. There will be differentiated booklets so that all pupils have materials at their level and also materials which will provide graded challenges.

ICT provision in languages will be matched to need. The department will use onscreen grids, word-processing packages, Internet, CD-ROM symbols and cause and effect software where appropriate to promote and extend the spoken and written language.

Behaviour

There will be a departmental reward system for all pupils. Pupils with SEN need to have their achievements recognised especially when progress is very slow.

Misbehaviour should be dealt with promptly. Pupils should have a maximum of two warnings before they are sent out of class.

Any problems or issues should be referred to the Head of Department.

SEN and Disability Act 2001 (SENDA)

1. The SEN and Disability Act 2001 amends the Disability Discrimination Act 1995 to include schools' and LEAs' responsibility to provide for pupils and students with disabilities.

2. The definition of a disability in this Act is:

   Someone who has a physical or mental impairment that has an effect on his or her ability to carry out normal day-to-day activities. The effect must be:

   - substantial (that is, more than minor or trivial); and

   - long term (that is, has lasted or is likely to last for at least a year or for the rest of the life of the person affected); and

   - adverse.

Activity: List any pupils that you come across who would fall into this category.

3. The Act states that the responsible body for a school must take such steps as it is reasonable to take to ensure that disabled pupils and disabled prospective pupils are not placed at substantial disadvantage in comparison with those who are not disabled.

Activity: Give an example of something which might be considered 'a substantial disadvantage'.

4. The duty on the school to make reasonable adjustments is anticipatory. This means that a school should not wait until a disabled pupil seeks admission to consider what adjustments it might make generally to meet the needs of disabled pupils.

Activity: Think of two reasonable adjustments that could be made in your school/department.

5. The school has a duty to plan strategically for increasing access to the school education, which includes provision of information for pupils and parents (e.g. Braille or taped versions of brochures), improving the physical environment for disabled students and increasing access to the curriculum by further differentiation.

Activity: Consider ways of increasing access to the school for a pupil requesting admission who has Down's Syndrome with low levels of literacy and a heart condition that affects strenuous physical activity.

6. Schools need to be proactive in seeking out information about a pupil's disability (by establishing good relationships with parents and carers, asking about disabilities during admission interviews etc.) and ensuring that all staff who might come across the pupil are aware of the pupil's disability.

Activity: List the opportunities that occur in your school for staff to gain information about disabled students. How can these be improved on?

INSET Activity A

Special Educational Need	Characteristics	Strategies
Attention Deficit Disorder – with or without hyperactivity	• has difficulty following instructions and completing tasks • easily distracted by noise, movement of others, attracting attention, objects • can't stop talking, interrupts others, calls out • acts impulsively without thinking about the consequences	• keep instructions simple – the one sentence rule • make eye contact and use the pupil's name when speaking to him • sit the pupil away from obvious distractions • provide clear routines and rules, rehearse them regularly
Autistic Spectrum Disorder	• may experience high levels of stress and anxiety when routines are changed • may have a literal understanding of language • more often interested in objects rather than people • may be sensitive to light, sound, touch or smell	• give a timetable for each day • warn the pupil about changes to usual routine • avoid using too much eye contact as it can cause distress • use simple clear language, avoid using metaphor, sarcasm
Down's Syndrome	• takes longer to learn and consolidate new skills • limited concentration • has difficulties with thinking, reasoning, sequencing • has better social than academic skills • may have some sight, hearing, respiratory and heart problems	• use simple familiar language • give time for information to be processed • break lesson up into a series of shorter, varied tasks • accept a variety of ways of recording work, drawings, diagrams, photos, video

Special Educational Need	Characteristics	Strategies
Hearing impairment	• hearing in right ear only • has a monaural loss	• check on the best seating position • check that the pupil can see your face for expressions and lip reading • indicate where a pupil is speaking from during class discussion, only allow one speaker at a time
Dyscalculia	• has a discrepancy between development level and general ability in maths • has difficulty counting by rote • misses out or reverses numbers • has difficulty with directions, left and right • loses track of turns in games, dance	• provide visual aids, number lines, lists of rules, formulae, words • encourage working out on paper • provide practical objects to aid learning

Instructions for activity

This activity should only take about ten minutes but can be used for additional discussion on strategies, concentrating on the easy ones to implement or the ones already being used.

1. Photocopy onto paper or card.

2. Cut the first column off the sheet.

3. Cut out the remaining boxes.

4. Either keep the two sets of boxes separate, firstly matching the characteristics then the strategies, or use all together.

Alternative activity

Make the boxes bigger with room for additional strategies or remove a couple of the strategies so staff can add any they have used or can identify.

INSET Activity B

Activity: What do we really think?

Each member of the department should choose two of these statements and pin them onto the noticeboard for an overview of staff opinion. The person leading the session (Head of Department, SENCO, senior manager) should be ready to address any negative feedback and take forward the department in a positive approach.

'If my own child had special needs, I would want her/him to be in a mainstream school mixing with all sorts of kids.'
_____

'I want to be able to cater for pupils with SEN but feel that I don't have the expertise required.'
_____

'Special needs kids in mainstream schools are all right up to a point, but I didn't sign up for dealing with the more severe problems – they should be in special schools.'
_____

'It is the SENCO's responsibility to look out for these pupils with SEN – with help from support teachers.'
_____

'Pupils with special needs should be catered for the same as any others. Teachers can't pick and choose the pupils they want to teach.'
_____

'I need much more time to plan if pupils with SEN are going to be coming to my lessons.'
_____

'Big schools are just not the right places for blind or deaf kids, or those in wheelchairs.'
_____

'I would welcome more training on how to provide for pupils with SEN in my subject.'
_____

'I have enough to do without worrying about kids who can't read or write.'
_____

'If their behaviour distracts other pupils in any way, youngsters with SEN should be withdrawn from the class.'

Case Studies

Read the case studies which follow. There are suggestions for classroom strategies here but there is also space for you to add your own.

Kuli Y8, Hearing impairment

Kuli has profound hearing loss. He has some hearing in his right ear but is heavily reliant on visual cues ranging from lip reading to studying body language and facial expression to get the gist and tone of what people are saying. He often misses crucial details. Reading is a useful alternative input and his mechanical reading skills are good, but he does not always get the full message because of language delay. He has problems with new vocabulary and with asking and responding to questions.

He follows the same timetable as the rest of his class for most of the week but he has some individual tutorial sessions with a teacher of the deaf to help with his understanding of the curriculum and to focus on his speech and language development. This is essential but it does mean that he misses some classes, so he is not always up to speed with a subject.

He has a good sense of humour but appreciates visual jokes, more than ones which are language based. He is very literal and is puzzled by all sorts of idioms. He was shocked when he heard that someone had been 'painting the town red' as he thought this was an act of vandalism! Even when he knows what he wants to say he does not always have the words or structures to communicate accurately what he knows.

Everyone is very pleasant and quite friendly to him but he is not really part of any group and quite often misunderstands what other children are saying. He has a Learning Assistant which again marks him out as different. He gets quite frustrated because he always has ideas that are too complex for his expressive ability. He can be very sulky and has temper tantrums.

Strategies

- Kuli needs to know what is coming up in the next few lessons so he can prepare the vocabulary and get some sense of the main concepts and thus be able to follow what is being said.

- A good TA will find ways of displaying information visually using drawings, pictures, signs, symbols, sign language, mime and animations on the computer, etc.

- ....

- ....

- ....

Bhavini Y9, Visual impairment

Bhavini has very little useful sight. She uses a stick to get around the large comprehensive school where she is a pupil, and some of the other children make cruel comments about this which she finds very hurtful. She also wears glasses with thick lenses which she hates. On more than one occasion, she has been knocked over in the corridor, but she insists that these incidents were accidents and that she is not being bullied. However, her sight is so poor she could not recognise anyone who picked on her.

She has a certain amount of specialist equipment such as talking scales in cookery, a CCTV for textbooks and is always conscious of being different. Her classmates accept her, but she is very cut off as she does not make eye contact or see well enough to find people she knows to sit with at break. She spends a lot of time hanging around the support area. Her form tutor has tried to get other children to take her under their wing or to escort her to humanities, which is in another building, but this has bred resentment. She has friends outside school at the local Phab club and has taken part in regional VI Athletics tournaments, but she opts out of sport at school if she can. Some of the teachers are concerned about health and safety issues and there has been talk about her being disapplied from science.

She has a reading age approximately three years behind her chronological age and spells phonetically. Many of the teaching strategies which are used to make learning more interesting disadvantage her. The lively layout of her French book with cartoons and speech bubbles is a nightmare. Even if she has a page on her CCTV or has a photocopy of the text enlarged she cannot track which bit goes where. At the end of one term she turned up at the support base asking for some work to do because 'they're all watching videos.'

Strategies

- Her isolation is the key factor and needs addressing most urgently.

- She needs to be put in groups with different pupils who will not overwhelm her.

- She needs work on spelling – core vocabulary and spelling patterns which are not phonic.

- ....

- ....

- ....

Megan Y10, Wheelchair user

Nicknamed Little Miss Angry, everyone knows when Megan is around! She is very outgoing, loud and tough. No one feels sorry for her – they wouldn't dare! Megan has spina bifida and needs personal care as well as educational support. She has upset a number of the less experienced classroom assistants who find her a real pain. Some of the teachers like her because she is very sparky. If she likes a subject, she works hard – or at least she did until this year.

Megan has to be up very early for her parents to help get her ready for school before the bus comes at 7.50 am. She lives out of town and is one of the first to be picked up and one of the last to be dropped off, so she has a longer school day than many of her classmates. Tiredness can be a problem as everything takes her so long to do and involves so much effort.

Now she is 15 she has started working towards her GCSEs and has the potential to get several A to Cs, particularly in maths and sciences. She is intelligent, but is in danger of becoming disaffected because everything is so much harder for her than for other children. Recently she has lost her temper with a teacher, made cruel remarks to a very sensitive child and turned her wheelchair round so she sat with her back to a supply teacher. She has done no homework for the last few weeks saying that she doesn't see the point as 'no one takes a crip seriously'.

Strategies

- Urgent support is needed to minimise the physical effort involved in writing and recording.

- The school needs to establish ground rules about behaviour.

- Rotate TAs so Megan doesn't wear them out.

- ....

- ....

- ....

Steven Y8, Emotional, behavioural, social difficulties

'Stevie' is a real charmer – sometimes! He is totally inconsistent: one day, he is full of enthusiasm; the next day, he is very tricky and he needs to be kept on target. He thrives on attention. In primary school, he spent a lot of time sitting by the teacher's desk and seemed to enjoy feeling special. If he sat there he would get on with his work, but as soon as he moved to sit with his friends he wanted to make sure he was the centre of attention.

Steven sometimes seems lazy looking for the easy way out but at other times he is quite dynamic and has lots of bright ideas. He can't work independently and has a very short attention span. No one has very high expectations of him and he is not about to prove them wrong.

Some of the children don't like him because he can be a bully but really he is not nasty. He is a permanent lieutenant for some of the tougher boys and does things to win their approval. He is a thief but mostly he takes silly things, designed to annoy rather than for any monetary value. He was found with someone's library ticket and stole one shoe from the changing rooms during PE.

Since his mother has taken up with a new partner, there has been a deterioration in behaviour and Steven has also been cautioned by police after stealing from a local DIY store. He has just been suspended for throwing a chair at a teacher but, staff suspect, this was because he was on a dare. He certainly knows how to get attention.

Strategies

- Steven needs a structured programme with lots of rewards – certificates, merits, etc.

- Praise to overcome negative self-image.

- ....

- ....

- ....

Matthew Y9, Cognitive and learning difficulties

Matt is a very passive boy. He has no curiosity, and no strong likes or dislikes. One teacher said, 'He's the sort of boy who says yes to everything to avoid further discussion but I sometimes wonder if he understands anything.'

He is quite a loner. He knows all the children and does not feel uncomfortable with any of them, but is always on the margins. Often in class he sits and does nothing, just stares into space. He is no trouble and indeed if there is any kind of conflict, he absents himself or ignores it. No one knows very much about him as he never volunteers any information. In French, he once said that he had a dog, and one teacher has seen him on the local common with a terrier, but no one is sure if it is his.

He does every piece of work as quickly as possible to get it over with. His work is messy and there is no substance to anything he does, which makes it hard for teachers to suggest a way forward, or indeed to find anything to praise. Matthew often looks a bit grubby and is usually untidy. He can be quite clumsy and loses things regularly but does not bother to look for them. He does less than the minimum.

He is in a low set for maths but stays in the middle. He has problems with most humanities subjects because he has no empathy and no real sense of what is required. When the class went to visit a museum for their work on the Civil War, he was completely unmoved. To him, it was just another building, and he could not really link it with the work they had done in history.

Strategies

- Involve him in pair work with a livelier pupil who will 'gee' him up a bit.

- Set up some one-to-one sessions with a TA where he is pushed to respond.

- Get him using technology to improve the appearance of his work, perhaps in a homework club after school.

- ....

- ....

Susan Y10, Complex difficulties, Autistic Spectrum Disorder

Susan is a tall, very attractive girl who has been variously labelled as having Asperger's and 'cocktail party syndrome'. She talks fluently but usually about something totally irrelevant. She is very charming and her language is sometimes quite sophisticated, but her understanding and ability to use language for school work operate at a much lower level. Her reading is excellent on some levels, but she cannot draw inferences from the printed word. If you ask her questions about what she has read, she looks blank, echoes what you have said, looks puzzled, or changes the subject – something she is very good at.

She finds relationships quite difficult. She is very popular, especially with the boys in her class. They think she is a laugh. There have been one or two problems with older boys in the school. Her habit of standing too close to people and her over-familiarity in manner have led to misunderstandings which have upset her badly. Her best friend Laura is very protective of her and tries to mother her, to the extent of doing some of her work for her so she won't get into trouble.

Her work is limited. In art, all her pictures look the same – very small cramped drawings – and she does not like to use paint because 'it's messy.' She finds it very hard to relate to the wider world and sees everything in terms of her own experience. The class has been studying *Macbeth* and she has not moved beyond saying, 'I don't believe in witches and ghosts'.

Some teachers think she is being wilfully stupid or not paying attention. She seems to be attention seeking as she is very poor at turn taking and shouts out in class if she thinks of something to say or wants to know how to spell a word. When she was younger, she used to retreat under the desk when she was upset and had to be coaxed out. She is still easily offended and cannot bear being teased. She has an answer for everything and, while it may not be sensible or reasonable, there is always an underlying logic.

Strategies

- Susan should be taught to count to 20 before opening her mouth.

- She should be given writing frames and model answers she can base her work on.

- There should be discussion of social issues, body language, appropriate behaviour, etc.

- ....

- ....

- ....

Jenny Y7, Down's Syndrome

Jenny is a very confident child who has been cherished and encouraged by her mother and older brothers and sisters. She is very assertive and is more than capable of dealing with spiteful comments: 'I don't like it when you call me names. You're cruel and I hate you', but this assertiveness can lead to obstinacy. She is prone to telling teachers that they are wrong!

She is good at reading and writing but her work is sometimes unimaginative and pedestrian. She enjoys maths and biology but finds the rest of the science curriculum hard going. She has started to put on weight and tries to avoid PE. She has persuaded her mother to provide a note saying that she tires easily but staff know that she is a bundle of energy and is an active member of an amateur theatre group which performs musicals. She has a good singing voice and enjoys dancing.

She went to a local nursery and primary school and fitted in well. She always had someone to sit next to and was invited to all the best birthday parties. Teachers and other parents frequently praised her, and she felt special.

Now, in secondary school, everything has changed. Some of her friends from primary school have made new friendships and don't want to spend so much time with her. She is very hurt by this and feels excluded. She is also struck by how glamorous some of the older girls look, and this has made her more self-conscious.

Strategies

- Talk to Jenny's parents about diet and exercise, and find a way of making her feel more attractive.

- Encourage new groupings in class so she gets to meet other children from different feeder schools.

- ....

- ....

- ....

Harry Y7, Dyslexia

Harry is a very anxious little boy and, although he has now started at secondary school, he still seems to be a 'little boy'. His parents have been very concerned about his slow progress in reading and writing and arranged for a dyslexia assessment when he was eight years old. They also employ a private tutor who comes to the house for two hours per week, and they spend time each evening and at weekends hearing him read and working on phonics with him.

Harry expresses himself well orally, using words which are very sophisticated and adult. His reading is improving (RA 8.4) but his handwriting and spelling are so poor that it is sometimes difficult to work out what he has written. He doesn't just confuse *b* and *d* but also *h* and *y*, *p* and *b*. Increasingly, he uses only a small bank of words that he knows he can spell.

His parents want him to be withdrawn from French on the grounds that he has enough problems with English. The French teacher reports that Harry is doing well with his comprehension and spoken French and is one of the more able children in the class.

Some staff get exasperated with Harry as he is quite clumsy, seems to be in a dream half the time, and cannot remember a simple sequence of instructions. He has difficulty telling left from right and so is often talking about the wrong diagram in a book or out of step in dance classes. 'He's just not trying,' said one teacher, while others think he needs 'to grow up a bit'.

He is popular with the girls in his class and recently has made friends with some of the boys in the choir. Music is Harry's great passion, but his parents are not willing for him to learn an instrument at the moment.

Strategies

- Find out how he has learnt things and see if similar strategies would work in the classroom.

- Investigate the possibility of using a computer with a spellchecker at home and school to cope with orthographic and spelling difficulties.

- ....

- ....

- ....

Whiteboards

There has been some research on this new technology which shows many of its positive features. Becta has information on the Virtual Teachers Centre (VTC): http://vtc.ngfl.gov.uk/

Advantages

- Pupils appear to be more interested in presentations using the board.
- Teachers make wider use of a variety of media, and lessons are more 'interactive'.
- The ability to create 'movement' on the board, through dragging and dropping text and pictures or using animation in software such as PowerPoint, is valuable to kinaesthetic learners and can aid the understanding of grammar.
- Students are keen to use this medium for their own presentations, enhancing their own oral and presentational skills.
- It is easier for all pupils to understand the processes underlying reading and writing when these skills are approached as whole-class activities via an electronic whiteboard. The focus provided by the whiteboard and the increased opportunities for interactivity with the text mean that the pupils are more fully engaged with the tasks.
- Teachers have access to a great range of resources – more than they would normally be able to use in a traditional classroom with no computer. It is useful to be able to open presentations that have already been delivered for revision purposes or to draw on a bank of resources saved on the computer or the school network.
- Transitions between different activities linked via an interactive whiteboard are smoother, as all the resources are readily to hand through a central point.

Considerations

- Is the board positioned so that it can easily be seen by everyone in the class?
- Can pupils use the board without standing in the beam?
- Is there a child who is reliant on lip reading? If so, arrange for them to sit near the front, in a position where they can see your mouth clearly. Make sure you stand where the light does not hide your face. They will need to see mouth shapes clearly if they are to have any hope of pronouncing the sounds.
- Is the text on the screen easy to read? Check the font size. Where teachers write additional notes on the screen as well, the text can become jumbled and hard to read.
- There are health and safety issues. Check cables are covered. This is especially important for pupils who are visually impaired.

Good and Bad Worksheets

A poor worksheet

Plan a day out

Pizza Lumière.

Tél. 895 54 87

Ouvert tous les jours

"C'est si bon!"

Restaurant Mirabeau

Tél 679.30.33 Plat du jour 20E; Fermé dimanche

CHEZ PIERRE

Tél 583 79.30. Déjeuner, dîner, souper. Fermé lundi et mardi. Fruits des mers et crustaces

Musée de l'Armée, Hôtel des invalides

Tél. 55 97 30

Ouvert tous les jours 10h á 19h Entrée 6 E

14h á 17 h films sur les deux guerres mondiales

"Merveilleux!"

What makes this hard to read?

- the irregular spacing between words and lines
- the right justified margin
- the range of fonts
- the range of font sizes
- the text wrapped around an image
- the use of italics and bold
- the mixture of capital letters and lower case
- the activity is not explained

These features would disadvantage a learner with poor visual tracking skills. A pupil with dyslexia, learning difficulties or lacking confidence would struggle with the layout . . . and that's before they start trying to make sense of the words! What are they supposed to do other than read the text?

A good worksheet

Lisez le texte suivant. Répondez aux questions.

Salut!

Je m'appelle Maria . . . Comment t'appelles tu? Je suis fille unique et j'ai quatorze ans. Je suis canadienne. Ma mère est australienne mais mon père est canadien. D'où viens tu? Je suis en troisième, c'est très difficile parce qu'il y a beaucoup de devoirs.

Pour mes passetemps j'aime parler au téléphone, faire du shopping, lire des livres romantiques, regarder des films d'horreur. J'aime aussi la natation et le soccer.

Ma musique preferée est le hip-hip et le rap.

Bon, maintement je dois aller à mon prochain cours.

Au revoir~!

Maria

	Vrai?	Faux?
Elle est espagnole	☐	☐
Elle aime la natation	☐	☐
Elle regard les films romantiques	☐	☐

What makes this a good worksheet?

- The use of two fonts: one for text, one for activities/instructions.
- Short lines and 1.5 line spacing helps with tracking.
- The activity is clear so the pupil knows what to do.

Pictures

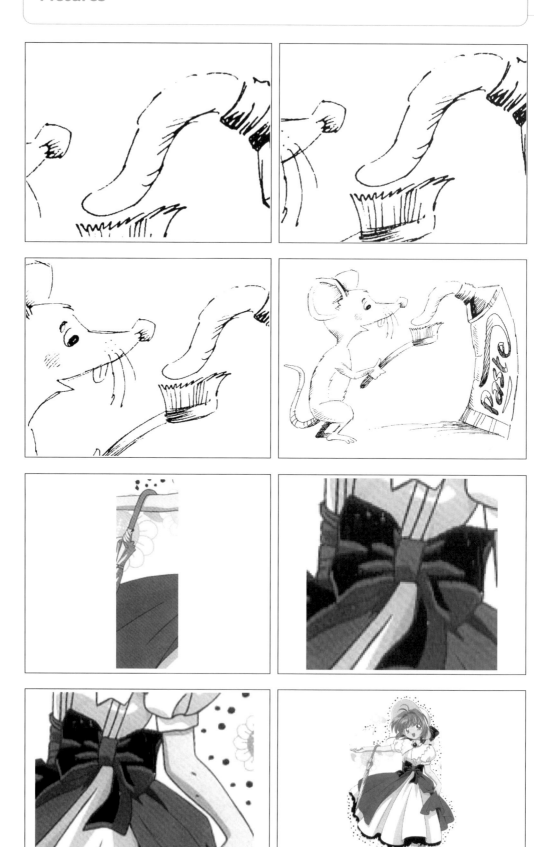

Resources

This is a selection of the most commonly used resources to encourage differentiation.

Software

Chatterbox Primary French http://www.sherston.com/

This is aimed at juniors but has lots to offer KS3 as well. It is a complete course in basic French that includes lesson plans, worksheets, flashcards, games and spoken activities.

Textease http//www.softease.com/

A talking word processing package with a library of pictures. Ideal for the MFL classroom as it has speech engine and spellchecker for French and German. This provides valuable support for pupils and is a good tool for developing resources. It also offers an easy way to insert and link words, pictures, sounds and video. Featured in a Becta MFL case study:

http://vtc.ngfl.gov.uk/docserver.php?docid=2163

There is a report on the Virtual Teachers Centre about using *Textease* to improve motivation among boys:
http://curriculum.becta.org.uk/docserver.php?docid=3729

Wordgames SPA http://www.spasoft.co.uk/

This package makes crosswords and word hunts from your own lists of words. Play on computer or print out on paper. See German examples in Appendix 6.1.

HyperStudio 4.1 from TAG http://www.taglearning.com/

This is a versatile and easy-to-use multimedia program. It allows pupils to create interactive presentations with linked pages that can contain text, photographs, video, sound and animations.

Clicker 4 from Crick Software http://www.cricksoft.com/

Clicker 4 is designed to support writing activities. The top half of the screen is a word processor page and the bottom half of the screen is a grid containing words and pictures. Children can type directly in the word processor area or click on the grid to insert words, phrases or pictures into their work. The software can be configured to read back text, and grids can be created to include sounds and videos. MFL samples available. The Clicker website offers a lot of support for teachers, and provides links for information about using Clicker effectively, and access to free ready-made Clicker Grid, an excellent teaching resource.

ClozePro from Crick Software http://www.cricksoft.com/

Provides a range of exciting and stimulating cloze activities. Children click on words to fill in gaps in sentences. You can also use it to create paper-based cloze activities very quickly and easily. Clicker Grids for Learning Cloze Pro and Clicker Grids submitted by practising teachers.
http://www.learninggrids.com/

TaskMagic Authoring Software http://www.mdlsoft.co.uk/

TaskMagic can be used for literacy or modern foreign languages activities and lets teachers make a whole suite of activities: gap filling, quizzes, matching picture and word, matching picture and sound. The program will then convert the activities into a range of games. It's useful for vocabulary building and communicative language skills and pupils will particularly enjoy the *Who Wants To Be A Millionaire?* games. You can download a demo version.

Fun with Texts Camsoft http://www.camsoftpartners.co.uk/

This is probably the best known text reconstruction program although the sample files are very academic.

The Authoring Suite Wida Software http://www.wida.co.uk/

An authoring program for teachers to create language activities on the computer including multimedia features. This can be purchased either as a whole or in parts. It contains several programs, including *Storyboard*, a text reconstruction program; *Gapmaster*, a cloze program; and *Matchmaster*, where the program jumbles up matching pairs of words or sentences, and the students have to match them up. Six different language games are generated by the computer from lists of keywords, definitions and example sentences entered by the teacher.

Developing Tray 2Simple Software
http://www.2simple.com/devtray/

This package gets its name from the fact that the text evolves in much the same way that a negative comes into focus in a photographer's developing tray. It can be successfully used with a wide variety of ages and abilities, from infant to adult.

Writing with Symbols 2000 Widgit http://www.widgit.com/

In Writing with Symbols, the menus and front screen remain in English, but at the click of a button, you can change the word lists, the spellchecker and the speech into French, Spanish or German. This program helps pupils relate words to concepts. A grid of accented letters makes writing easier for students who can type. The speech engines let pupils become familiar with pronunciation.

CD-ROMs

Talk Now EuroTalk http://www.eurotalk.com/

Covers first words; phrases; food; shopping; numbers and time; monitors pupils' progress; pupils can compare their pronunciation with native speakers.

Ecoutez Bien EuroTalk

Interactive quizzes and exercises to practise elementary listening skills in French, with a recording feature for pronunciation practice. Situations include shopping, restaurants, and leisure. Two disks are available.

En Route (French) Unterwegs (German) En Marcha (Spanish) AVP Computing http://avp.100megs28.com/

Differentiated activities; topics include hobbies, transport, and weather.
Interactive exercises use video and audio materials.

French Grammar Studio Granada Learning
http://www.granada-learning.com/

Standalone program for practising grammar skills. Has photo stories and the Grammar Factory.

The Games Box Usable Software Company
www.usablesoftwarecompany.com/

Authoring games and language learning. Over 20 games for French or Spanish; a large number of five to ten-minute activities suitable for pairwork or whole-class activity.

Taskmaster MDL http://www.mdlsoft.co.uk/

Many types of interactive games: Text Match, Picture Match, Sound Match, Pic Sound Match, Multiple Choice, Mix and Gap, Dialogues. Within each game there is a variety of interactive activities which give them a 'score' for the level of understanding.

Who Is Oscar Lake? Camsoft Ltd
http://www.camsoftpartners.co.uk/

Available for French, German, Italian, Spanish. Involves listening, looking and doing. A mystery story set in an everyday town with real people, with video scenes running under QuickTime. Book train tickets, hand the ticket clerk the money, pick up your ticket and put it in your briefcase! Develops a 1,200 word vocabulary. Voice record/playback feature. Save the game at any point.

Good websites

- Bonjour (http://www.bonjour.org.uk/), produced by The Howard School in Rainham, is an interesting site which has won many awards. It covers many of the areas needed for KS3 and 4 such as Moi et ma famille, La Vie au quotidien, Mon environment, Le monde du travail.

- Website reviews and fantastic photos http://www.ashcombe.surrey.sch.uk/

- Ros Walker is an independent trainer. Her site has lots of useful resources and practical ideas http://www.ros.org.uk/mfl/

- Zut http://www.zut.org.uk/ Over 400 interactive activities including more than 100 natively spoken sound files. Several activities have been specifically adapted for use with the electronic whiteboard and there are several topical and seasonal quizzes and lesson starter ideas.

Organisations

- CILT, the Centre for Information on Language Teaching and Research, 20, Bedfordbury, London WC2 4LB Tel: 020 7879 5101. http://www.cilt.org.uk/ Vital information for MFL teachers.

- Linguanet ICT and online resources http://www.linguanet.org.uk/

- ALL is now the major subject association for those involved in teaching modern foreign languages (MFL) at all levels and in all languages. http://www.languagelearn.co.uk/aboutall.htm

- Teacher Resource Exchange http://tre.ngfl.gov.uk/ The Teacher Resource Exchange is a moderated database of resources and activities designed to help teachers develop and share ideas for good practice. Lots of really good resources to download and use.

- Becta *SAY IT* gives a round-up of computer terminology in 28 languages including French, German, Spanish, Japanese and Welsh. http://www.becta.org.uk/teachers/teachers.cfm?section=1_3_1&id=2625 Becta has an MFL and Special Needs site at KS3. http://curriculum.becta.org.uk/ docserver.php?docid=3765&output register has material on the family, where we live, hobbies and interests, using on-screen word-grids.

- Virtual Teachers Centre http://vtc.ngfl.gov.uk/uploads/text/ sen_intro-29157.pdf has an introduction to MFL and SEN which covers family, hobbies and where we live.

Images

- http://www.ablestock.com This site has wonderful colour photographs. You type in a word and the search engine produces lots of pictures which fit your key word.

- Royalty-Free Clip Art Collection for Foreign/Second Language Instruction at http://www.sla.purdue.edu/fll/japanproj/flclipart/.

Miscellaneous

See it Right

RNIB has published a pack of information about providing information in accessible formats. Called the *See it Right* pack, it consists of 12 booklets, each dealing with a different aspect of accessible information. Details about the *See it Right* pack can be found on the RNIB website at www.rnib.org.uk/seeitright/.

Talking Dice http://www.talkingdice.co.uk/

A new and popular game to develop and improve speaking and listening skills. Can be used with any language but activities geared to MFL National Curriculum topics. Teachers feel it helps with drilling vocabulary, grammar, sentence building, story telling and discussion.

Coloured acetate overlays are available for materials printed on white paper. They are available from Cerium Visual Technologies, Cerium Technology Park, Appledore Road, Tenterton, Kent TN30 7DE. Tel: 01580 765211. http://www.ceriumvistech.co.uk. Email: ceriumgrp@aol.com. Packs of five A4 overlays (which can be all one colour or a mixture) cost £14.98 per pack including VAT and postage. A testing set containing two sets of each colour (A5 size) and guidelines for use is available for £51.88. A testing set enables the student to decide which colour is best for them – this is very much down to the individual.

Starter Activities

Starter activities tune pupils into the language and get them thinking and working. Keep them short. Beware any starters that involve anagrams or rearranging letters within part of a word. These are not suitable for pupils with dyslexia or others who have poor visual spelling skills.

Wordworms to recognise words and improve vocabulary

JeanetPierrerentrentchezeuxaprèsunemoisdevacancesàlacampagne
Jean et Pierre rentrent chez eux après une mois de vacances à la campagne.

Reorganise words within a sentence to develop a sense of syntax

Die Ferien:
anschauen. / Markt / den / Ich / will /
Wir / wollen / Fahrräder / leihen.

Match up words and topics to recognise contexts (Look for key words)

Palabras	Lugares
1. No me siento bien.	a. el banco
2. La cuenta por favor.	b. la piscina
3. Tiene usted un plan de la ciudad?	c. la farmacia
4. A qué hora empieza la pelicula?	d. el restaurante
5. Querría cambiar dinero.	e. información y turismo
6. El agua está fría.	f. el cine

(Answers 1c, 2d, 3e, 4f, 5a, 6b)

Find the odd one out to practise grammar/vocabulary

rot/grau/klein/gelb   (klein not a colour)
Allemagne anglais chinois espagnol   (Allemagne country/nationalities)
singen/zwei/kaufen/zahlen   (zwei not a verb)
correos buzón sellos reloj   (reloj not to do with Post Office)

Fill in missing letters to practise spelling and revise vocabulary

Strong verbs with haben:

   b- -i-nen   (beginnen)

   s- -en   (sehen)

   -e-men   (nehmen)

   -r-n-en   (trinken)

Match beginning and ends of sentences – reading for sense

Ich habe ein Brüder.	Sie heißen Karl, Dieter und Hans.
Ich habe eine Schwester.	Sie heißen Ingrid und Erika.
Ich habe zwei Gebrüder und ein Halbbrüder.	Er heißt Hans.
Ich habe zwei Schwestern.	Sie heißen Michael und Elisabeth.
Ich habe ein Brüder und eine Halbschwester.	Sie heißt Gisela.

Find the grammatical mistakes

Adjectival agreements:

Marie a perdu les chemises blanc.   (blanches)

J'ai acheté des chaussures verts.   (vertes)

La jupe noir est trop courts.   (noire, courte)

Odd sound out to practise pronunciation and to match sound to spelling

Michelle; chercher; chez; glace; riche   (glace)

Quand; jusque; cher; pourquoi; quelle   (cher)

Bois; noir; doux; choisir; pourquoi   (doux)

Jambon; chaise; bonjour; bijou; ajouter   (chaise)

French Vocabulary Work

1 Adjectives

1. You are working on adjectives to describe people. The class has a core of 20 basic adjectives.

aimable	amusant	bavard	beau	charmant
chic	dangereux	difficile	drôle	ennuyeux
génial	gentil	honnête	intelligent	joli
mignon	paresseux	poli	sportif	sympathique

Choose two of the following activities.

(a) Choose a character from a soap. (Give them one if the decision making is going to go on too long.) Pick out all the adjectives which apply to him or her. Find three other adjectives which could apply to that person.

(b) Draw a wanted poster. Avez-vous vu cet homme/cette femme?

(c) Pick three different people in the class. Create a form – nom /âge/cheveux/ yeux/caractère and fill in a form with four adjectives for each.

(d) Write a series of five questions which can be answered with YES /NO. Ton frère est parasseux? Est-il sportif?

2. Les smileys

This activity (created by Gail Haythorne of Woldingham School, Surrey) is from the Teachers' Resource Exchange http://tre.ngfl.gov.uk/
Vous chattez? Trouvez la bonne image pour chaque adjectif!

1. :-D	triste
2. :-0	très triste
3. ;-j	étonné/étonnée
4. >:->	rebelle
5. :c	fâché/fâchée
6. :-T	effrayé/effrayée
7. :*(	honnête
8. :-x	bavard/bavarde
9. :-P	heureux/heureuse
10. =:O	jeune
11. 0:)	impatient/impatiente
12. :()	ennuyé/ennuyée
13. :0)	timide
14. :-@	sarcastique
15. ~:)	irrité/irritée
16. l-0	méchant/méchante
17. :-}	gentil/gentille
18. :-[	embarrassé/embarrassée

Maintenant, décrivez votre famille et vos amis. Par exemple: Ma mère est heureuse et bavarde. Mon frère est souvent irrité.

Trouvez/inventez d'autres smileys. Recherchez 'Emoticons' dans le site: www.about.com

---

Les réponses: triste 5; très triste 7; étonné 2; rebelle 9; fâché 14; effrayé 10; honnête 11; bavard 12; heureux 1; jeune 15; impatient 6; ennuyé 16; timide 8; sarcastique 3; irrité 18; méchant 4; gentil 13; embarrassé 17

3. Remplissez les blancs

Cher/Chère _____

Ca va? Moi, ça va bien. Aujourd'hui je te parle un peu de mon collège. Mon collège s'appelle _____. Il y a _____ élèves. Moi, je suis en _____.

J'aime/je déteste le collège. J'aime (anglais, histoire etc.) _____ et _____, mais je n'aime pas _____ ou _____ (anglais, histoire, etc.) parce que _____.

Et toi, qu'est-ce que tu aimes au collège? Tu aimes les profs?

Écris-moi bientôt.

_____

4. Qu'est-ce que tu peux voir?

Testing German Vocabulary

Make word searches for different levels of ability, using Wordsquares software from SPA (www.spasoft.co.uk).

Differentiate word squares by:

- size (a smaller square with fewer words for an easier puzzle)

- checklist (provide the list of words to be found and matched – in English or German)

- orientation (letters running backwards or diagonally make the task more difficult)

Also, ask the pupils to make up their own word search.

How many German words can you find?

```
G S S T R A N D R B J W R L K
I P F G R C T Z F X G A Z W K
Z B O S C H U L E S A S X A N
P S D R E P N N O A L R F L O
E E F R M W D Y S T A D T D X
C E M W P S C H W I M M B A D
E X S C O K Q P B R R A Q G B
T L P H O T E L S R Z W G E U
N U S L A C I P J J F U A I R
M Q R T V S A P V U J K X Q G
Z D M M F L U G H A F E N U F
K Z A M A R K T L G D F J K Y
C A M P I N G P L A T Z Z Z X
K I N O K I R C H E C P L V O
O S U H Q P L B A H N H O F E
```

Different Intelligences Most Closely Linked to MFL

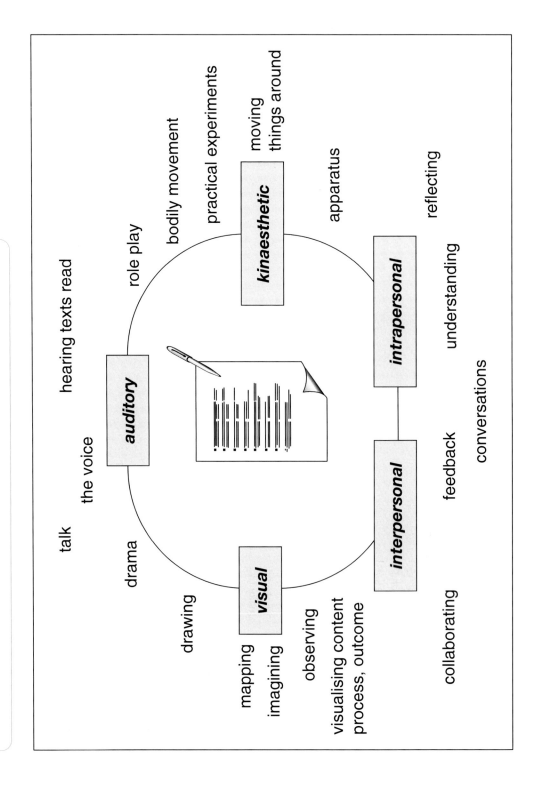

Table of Alternative Qualifications

Board	Qualification	Details	Contact
AQA	GNVQ Language Units at KS4	*Languages:* French, German and Spanish ● Equivalent to a GCSE Short Course ● Based on the National Curriculum Areas of Experience C and D ● Foundation Level (broadly equivalent to half a GCSE grade G–D) ● Intermediate Level (broadly equivalent to half a GCSE C–A*) Each unit has two elements: ☐ oral communication: speaking; listening and responding; ☐ written communication: writing; reading and responding. Candidates are awarded a Pass or Fail in each element and require a Pass in both elements in order to be awarded a Pass for the unit. The elements are assessed internally and externally through externally set tests and there is a coursework component. A portfolio is not required. Candidates must pass Oral and Written Communication to satisfy National Curriculum requirements, but the units may be accredited separately.	AQA (Assessment & Qualifications Alliance) 31–33 Springfield Avenue, Harrogate, North Yorkshire HG1 2HW Tel: 01423 840 015. Fax: 01423 523 678 Website: http://www.aqa.org.uk
AQA	Certificate of Achievement	*Languages:* French, German and Spanish Aimed at candidates expected to achieve below GCSE grade G. Twelve units of work of which six must be completed. Each unit can be accredited separately as the course proceeds, provided the Centre is participating in the Unit Award Scheme. Otherwise, certification is at the end of the (normally two-year) course, which is teacher-assessed with moderation by the Board. 50% of the assessment is based on material provided by the Board. The course is based on the National Curriculum orders for KS4 and two-way transfer with GCSE courses is possible. Final entry date can be the same as for GCSE. *Note:* The pupils are 16 when they are entered and would have followed a GCSE course or a lower language course.	AQA (Assessment & Qualifications Alliance) 31–33 Springfield Avenue, Harrogate, North Yorkshire HG1 2HW Tel: 01423 840 015. Fax: 01423 523 678 Website: http://www.aqa.org.uk

Board	Qualification	Details	Contact
AQA/SEG	Certificate of Achievement	*Language:* French Aimed at pupils for whom GCSE is not appropriate. Based on Levels 1–3 of the National Curriculum and can be co-taught with GCSE Foundation Tier. The topic areas also reflect the content of GCSE syllabuses of other examination groups. The syllabus is split into four units and 15 weeks of teaching time per unit are recommended. The four attainment targets are tested and equally weighted. Speaking and Writing are assessed by coursework.	AQA/SEG Stag Hill House, Guildford, Surrey GU2 5XJ Tel: 01483 506 506. Fax: 01483 300 152
ASDAN	Bronze, Silver and Gold Award		
ASDAN	International Award		
ASDAN	Transition Challenge	*Languages:* any language An Entry Level programme for students with complex and severe learning difficulties. It is related to KS4 Programmes of Study but also to post-16 core skills. Five modules, which encapsulate the aims of personal development and independent living, are broken down into a set of 12 activities or subjects, from which the student chooses eight. MFL is one of the activities and offers provision for SEN students who have moved into KS4 and are looking to the world beyond school.	ASDAN Central Office, 27 Redland Hill, Bristol BS6 6UX Tel: 0117 946 6228. Fax: 0117 946 7668 Website: http://www.asdan.co.uk Contact: Roger White – Tel: 0117 923 9843
Birmingham Comenius Centre	Certificate of Achievement in MFL	*Languages:* French, German and Spanish The Certificate provides accreditation of achievement equivalent to National Curriculum Levels 1–3 and allows progression to later studies via GCSE of a vocational route. It is based on National Curriculum and GCSE requirements. The four skills are tested throughout ten units by a combination of coursework and end-of-unit assessment. Candidates complete seven or more units and count best unit marks. Assessment materials are provided but Centres can produce their own units and submit them for approval. This programme can be followed as a short or full course over one or two years. Certification is available at three levels.	Birmingham Comenius Centre Martineau Centre, Balden Road, Harborne, Birmingham, B32 2EH Tel: 0121 303 1190. Fax: 0121 303 1196 Contact: Paul Nutt – Tel: 0121 303 8146

Edexcel	Certificate of Achievement	*Languages:* French, German and Spanish This Certificate offers accreditation of achievement at National Curriculum Levels 1–3 but is flexible enough to accommodate work at a higher level. The scheme covers the five KS4 Areas of Experience, allowing two-way transfer, where appropriate between Certificate courses and those leading to GCSE. Assessment is done in class and the assessment tasks are externally set and moderated. There is a strong emphasis on coursework and the Board's Assessment Pack available from Edexcel Publications provides a bank of tasks covering the four skills. There is no end-of-year examination and teachers may select the assessment tasks that best fit their scheme of work. Certification is available at three levels. It is an Entry Level qualification.	Stewart House, 32 Russell Square, London WC1B 5DN Tel: 0870 240 9800. Fax: 020 7758 6960 Website: http://www.edexcel.org.uk
Edexcel	GNVQ Language Units at KS4	*Languages:* French, German and Spanish Foundation Level and Intermediate Level. A qualification in its own right with a vocational aim covering two Areas of Experience: the World around Us and the World of Work. There are two units per level: Oral and Written Communication. Foundation is broadly equivalent to half a GCSE grade G–D and Intermediate is broadly equivalent to half a GCSE grade C–A*. The units meet the National Curriculum requirements at KS4 when taken together but they can be taken individually. Students achieving only one unit receive a certificate for it. The elements are assessed internally and externally through externally set tests and there is a coursework component. A portfolio is not required. Future developments: as part of the KS4 review, this accreditation route is due to be revised with the intention of offering an Advanced Level of this qualification.	Edexcel Stewart House, 32 Russell Square, London WC1B 5DN Tel: 0870 240 9800. Fax: 020 7758 6960 Website: http://www.edexcel.org.uk

Board	Qualification	Details	Contact
OCR	Entry Level Certificate	*Languages:* French, German and Spanish This qualification has been designed to meet the needs of candidates who would be unlikely to achieve a grade at GCSE. The specification aims to meet the needs of candidates unable to cope with the demands of a GCSE examination. These would include some candidates who have received at least part of their teaching in Special Schools or in Departments of Special Educational Needs. They are also suitable to be run as a one-year course and may provide a stepping stone for possible progression to GCSE or equivalent. There are three pass grades (Entry 1, Entry 2 and Entry 3) which are broadly equivalent to the requirements for National Curriculum Levels 1, 2 and 3 and recognise a level of achievement below that of a grade G at GCSE.	OCR (Oxford, Cambridge & RSA Examinations) Westwood Way, Coventry CV4 8HS Tel: 02476 470 033. Fax: 02476 468 080 Website: http://www.ocr.org.uk
WJEC	Certificate of Educational Achievement	*Languages:* French, German and Spanish National Entry Level Award. The syllabus is designed to give pupils in the 14 $^+$ age group the opportunity to study a language. It is suitable for those who would not at the outset of the course be expected to attain a grade G at GCSE. It targets pupils who have not reached Level 3 of the National Curriculum at the end of their study of a MFL at Key Stage 3. It is a pathway to GCSE and links with GNVQ at Foundation Level. The scheme is assessed continuously to enable learners to display achievement in the four Attainment Targets: Listening and Responding, Speaking, Reading and Responding and Writing. The work is divided into ten units and there is no summative examination. The WJEC issues a Completion Certificate that may be awarded at the end of each unit and produces exercise booklets for each language. Practice material is also available for purchase.	WJEC (Welsh Joint Education Committee) 245 Western Avenue, Cardiff CF5 2YX Tel: 029 2026 5000. Fax: 029 2057 5994

Relationships Between Teacher and LSA – Issues for Discussion

- What will you expect from the Learning Assistant?

- Do all the MFL staff have a clear understanding of the roles and responsibilities of the LSA?

- What can they reasonably ask an LSA to do?

- Will he/she be expected to work with groups or individuals?

- What will be the status of the Teaching Assistant?

- How are Teaching Assistants referred to?

- Are pupils expected to treat them with the same degree of respect as they would a teacher?

- Should they suggest and make additional materials?

- Do you want them to write in pupils' books? If so, should it be in a different colour?

- Are LSAs responsible for care needs?

- Will the LSA be involved in planning?

- How will he/she feed back information about pupils' progress?

- Does he/she understand the importance of confidentiality?

- Will there be regular meetings between the HoD and LSA?

- Will they be expected to attend staff meetings?

- Should they provide written notes which could be incorporated into an IEP?

- Are LSAs responsible for setting up computers and finding other specialist equipment?

- Will opportunities be provided for him/her to become familiar with the hardware, software and teaching needs?

- Will training be available?

- Will support materials be provided?

Guidance for Teaching Assistants

Golden rules

- Help pupils to succeed but allow them to fail.

- In language learning, everyone learns from their mistakes.

- Avoid highly idiomatic English. Idioms are confusing for non-native speakers of English and for pupils with certain language disorders.

Personal information

- Build on and respect personal information and experience.

- In MFL classes you will learn a lot about people's identity, family – or lack of it, preferences, hobbies and lifestyle.

- MFL is very person-centred. Listen, learn and use this knowledge to foster closer relationships with the child.

- Beware differences in culture. Use a range of examples rather than ones which assume a particular background or experience. Not all pupils want shopping, music, reading or football as their hobbies.

Encourage pupils to participate in class but be aware of individual differences

- Don't just talk: draw and mime as well.

- Many pupils benefit from both seeing and hearing language.

- Try to get each pupil to participate in spoken work; ask questions but increase the time you wait for an answer for slower thinkers and less confident pupils.

- Challenge the louder and more dominant pupils.

- Don't assume that students who don't talk don't know the material.

- Think about talking to very quiet and very loud pupils outside class.

Managing Staff

Do you:

- ❑ share relevant information with LSAs?

- ❑ know the strengths that individual LSAs have?

- ❑ provide opportunities for these to be used in your lessons?

- ❑ provide opportunities for LSAs to meet others involved in children's learning, e.g. parents, speech therapist, educational psychologist?

- ❑ involve LSAs in pupil observations, development, etc.?

- ❑ provide opportunities for LSAs to contribute to planning?

- ❑ explain how LSAs can support the implementation of the schools' policies, e.g. behaviour management and bullying?

- ❑ schedule regular meetings with LSAs as a group, to address any issues of concern, for example lack of homework?

- ❑ help LSAs to review their own work?